Praise for *Every Body Beloved*

"God loves fat! And *Every Body Beloved* rings out with that same Divine love. Bromberg invites us into a lush, abundant world of Torah, poetry, story, and prayer celebrating the miracle of fatness. A future of chairs without arms, dance floors that welcome our ampleness, and Jewish communities that do not shy away from combating sizeism and fatphobia."

—Rabbi Ariana Katz, coauthor of *For Times Such as These* (Wayne State University Press)

"Rabbi Bromberg's generosity of spirit and erudite insights into Jewish text give a grounded and deeply compassionate alternative to perfectionist body loathing in our Ozempic era. This book is a high-leverage ethical tool in the work of affirming the sacredness of every body."

—Hanne Blank Boyd, author of *Fat* and *Straight: The Surprisingly Short History of Heterosexuality*

"Bromberg delivers a powerful and unflinching approach to embodiment that speaks not only to the mind but also to the spirit. She demonstrates the sacred reclaiming of our own stories, including fatness, holiness, and taking up literal and metaphorical space. This is a book for anyone who desires to unlearn shame, embrace joy, and celebrate the miracle of embodiment."

—Amy K. Milligan, Batten Endowed Associate Professor of Jewish Studies, Old Dominion University

"In *Every Body Beloved*, Minna brings her deep knowledge of the Torah that she loves so much, keen sociological observations, and heartfelt personal insights, weaving these together to create an innovative midrash that will entice readers both within the Jewish world and beyond."

—Melila Hellner Eshed, professor of Jewish mysticism and the Zohar, Hebrew University in Jerusalem

EVERY BODY BELOVED

Every Body Beloved

A JEWISH EMBRACE OF FATNESS

MINNA BROMBERG

Wayne State University Press

Detroit

© 2025 by Minna Bromberg. All rights reserved. No part of this book may be reproduced without formal permission.

ISBN 9780814352113 (paperback)
ISBN 9780814352120 (ebook)

Library of Congress Control Number: 2025931234

On cover: *Be Gentle with You* by Kat Max. Used by permission. @katmaxisfree on social media platforms; prints available. Cover design by Lindsey Cleworth.

Wayne State University Press rests on Waawiyaataanong, also referred to as Detroit, the ancestral and contemporary homeland of the Three Fires Confederacy. These sovereign lands were granted by the Ojibwe, Odawa, Potawatomi, and Wyandot Nations, in 1807, through the Treaty of Detroit. Wayne State University Press affirms Indigenous sovereignty and honors all tribes with a connection to Detroit. With our Native neighbors, the press works to advance educational equity and promote a better future for the earth and all people.

Wayne State University Press
Leonard N. Simons Building
4809 Woodward Avenue
Detroit, Michigan 48201-1309

Visit us online at wsupress.wayne.edu.

*For my children, beloved beyond measure.
I will gladly dance with you always,
wherever and however we like.*

Contents

You, Beloved

1

Introduction:
Broadcasting the Miracle of Fat

3

To my seven-year-old self

15

1. From Narrowness to Freedom

19

To my doctor who was proud of me for not having gestational diabetes

51

2. Fatness and the Divine Image
55

To the kid who drew a picture of me
to hurt my daughter's feelings
87

3. Taking Good Care
91

To the people at Yom Kippur services
who would not move to let me through
115

4. Making Space:
Chairing Is Caring
119

To the rabbi whose congregants were upset
about gaining weight
147

5. As We Love Ourselves

151

To my college boyfriend who broke up with me because I was fat and Jewish

177

6. Desiring Fat

183

Conclusion:
Opening to the Beloved

209

Acknowledgments

219

Notes

223

Works Cited

227

You, Beloved

You,
Beloved
are
Every body

Your voice in our every breath
Your light, the sparkle in our eyes
Your sweetness in our own kisses
Your saltiness, our tears

A touch of our hands,
the brush of your wings

Not a single cell devoid of you
Not a single fold unholy
Every single limb or lack thereof
another of your contours

Ample
Abundant
Ever
Is your image imprinted
Your oneness reflected in our all

In the body that is ill or aching
In the body derided and despised
In the body persevering and rejoicing

In the body
sometimes broken
always whole

Always you, Beloved
in every body

Every
Body
Beloved

Introduction
Broadcasting the Miracle of Fat

Dancing! I was meant to be dancing. Usually I would be perfectly happy with the fact that this was the first thing on the agenda at the preschool Chanukah party I was attending with my then-three-year-old daughter. We had walked into the synagogue sanctuary to find it teeming with dozens of overjoyed preschoolers and their parents. The music was just about to start!

I am a fat woman who uses the word "fat" as an accurate and morally neutral way of lovingly describing the size and shape of my body. I have been involved in fat activism for over thirty years, and that whole time, I have been practicing accepting myself as I am. Like any relationship, my relationship with my own body has its ups and downs, but I am usually, gratefully, pretty comfortable in my own skin. So, dancing in public with preschool children?!? Bring it on!

But that December, I was also thirty-nine-weeks pregnant and I wasn't really feeling up for anything so vigorous. When the songs started, I focused on doing my best to tenderly attend to my body, to gently listen to what I could or could not do right then physically. I let myself sway in time to the music, as I tried to stay in the moment with my very pregnant body and my very excited daughter. However, when she made it clear that she fully expected me to jump up and down with her, I suddenly felt defeated.

Waves of self-consciousness and judgment washed over me as I noticed this internal dialogue start up unbidden in my head. One voice said, "I hope everybody here knows that I'm pregnant and that's why I'm not jumping up and down." And then another chimed in: "Why am I using my pregnancy to try to defend myself against imagined fatphobic and ableist put-downs about my ever so slightly limited mobility? As if anyone in this context is actually going to say something judgmental about my fat body dancing?!?"

Spoiler alert: Someone was about to actually say something judgmental about fat bodies dancing.

The preschool had hired a young man to play guitar and lead the singing and dancing. I thought he was doing a lovely job. As a rabbi who is also a singer and a songwriter, I've been in his shoes, and playing music for a large gathering of youngsters can be quite a challenge. But he was putting in all the requisite energy to engage a roomful of little kids. After a few lively renditions of familiar Chanukah tunes, we took a break to eat *sufganiyot*.

I felt relieved that I could stop disappointing my daughter with my inability to jump up and down. Kids and parents alike were served the fried, jelly-filled Chanukah pastries. An absorbed hush fell over the munching crowd.

Soon, the young man picked up his guitar again, and once again I was impressed: he knew how to work with this age group well enough to bring them back into the music before anyone started wandering off. And that's when he check, check, checked his mic and said, "Okay! Let's all get back to dancing, unless you've gotten too fat from those *sufganiyot*!"

My son wouldn't be born until the following week, in a planned Cesarean birth, but with that song leader's one anti-fat quip, I felt as if my waters broke in a huge gush and I went into the long labor that would eventually birth this book. Up until that moment, I had mostly kept my fat activism separate from my work as a rabbi. I was suddenly unwilling to keep quiet anymore.

My father tells a story about one of his first calls when he began volunteering with the local ambulance. The call came in to help someone who had fallen from a ladder, and off he and his crew sped. The ambulance parked, my dad grabbed his gear, and he began running toward the person lying on the ground. At which point he saw that the patient had suffered a truly gruesome injury. My father had all the training he needed and was fully qualified to provide treatment. He had been drilled on a whole variety of scenarios. Yet in that moment, as he took in the gory scene, the thought that screamed through his head was "Good God, somebody call an ambulance!"

Hearing the sentence "Let's all get back to dancing, unless you've gotten too fat from those *sufganiyot*"—especially uttered in front of these sweet young kids—made me want to shout for somebody to call an emergency response team. Surely there was someone who would swoop in to put a stop to the injurious anti-fat bias being voiced here! Where were they?!? And then I realized that I was the person who had been called to respond. I had been teaching Torah, and I had been embracing fatness; now it was time to teach a Torah that embraces fatness.

I was hurt by the song leader's words. No matter how much body confidence I have personally, no matter how many decades I have practiced accepting myself and advocating for equal treatment for people of all sizes, it hurts to hear bodies like mine denigrated so easily and casually and publicly. People who live in despised bodies are expected to somehow laugh off these passing slights. But they happen so frequently and with so little compunction that it makes every social interaction a high-risk situation. And, at least for me, it hurts every single time. Every joke. Every unsolicited piece of weight-loss advice. Every bit of weird cheerleading for being "brave" enough to exercise in public, or eat in public, or wear a bathing suit in public, or just exist as a fat person in public.

There is a popular adage that we should "write from our scars and not from our wounds." I feel blessed to be able to share my own journey in these pages, including the healing I have experienced in my own relationship with my body. At the same time, those of us in bodies that are constantly degraded do not have the luxury of sharing wisdom only from the places in which we are already fully healed. The damage inflicted on us is not in the past; it is ongoing.

My own wounded heart is my main informant in this work. I am sharing the stories, experiences, and perspectives that are mine to share. And I know that readers will arrive to these pages with bodies, identities, and lifetimes of their own. I am a white, Ashkenazi, Gen X, temporarily able-bodied, somewhat straight woman who grew up in the United States and now lives in Jerusalem. In addition to being fat, I sometimes also identify as superfat, a designation that refers not to my superpowers but to a size of body that faces significant barriers to accessing seating, clothing, appropriately sized medical equipment, and so on.

What I am offering in these pages is not *the* Jewish embrace of fatness but *my* Jewish embrace of fatness. This is one rabbi's journey toward freedom from anti-fat bias. I share it in hopes that others will join me and lend their own unique viewpoints.

You too are reading this book from your own set of perspectives, in your own body, with its many interwoven roles, experiences, and identities—both those identities you claim for yourself and those that others read onto you, whether you like it or not. Each of our identities interacts with one another, and whatever combination of privilege and marginalization we carry influences how anti-fat bias impacts us.

Fatness also interacts not only with our actual Jewish bodies but also with stereotypes of Jewish bodies. Undeniably, some Jewish populations include folks who look alike. Some of us take pride in how our Jewishness is written on our bodies, while others have experienced this as stigmatizing. As a global multiracial, multiethnic people, shaped—and enriched—by conversion, adoption, and intermarriage, Jews come in all sorts of bodies, and there truly is no such thing as "the Jewish body." I have chosen to shy away from reifying various stereotypes of what Jews look like. Examining all the ways that Jewish identity has intersected with fatness would indeed be a very rich exploration. However, doing it justice is beyond both the scope and the aim of this book.

When I began more publicly sharing a Torah of fat liberation in 2020, Fat Torah emerged as an organization. Since then we have been offering workshops, teacher trainings, and consulting to communities and organizations that are ready to learn more about our approach to confronting anti-fatness. Through this work, I have spoken with hundreds of people about the impact of fatphobia in their lives and on their Judaism. My understanding of the need that this book meets has been shaped by these conversations. Along with my firsthand experiences, I share some of their stories here as well.

In addition to my own story, and the stories of those in my Fat Torah community, I also share plenty of examples of people behaving in ways that reveal their anti-fat bias. These are stories of real incidents involving real people, recounted as best I remember them. I am not trying to shame or hurt individuals who behaved or spoke in fatphobic ways. I bring these stories because they reflect some of my own experiences, but there is nothing particularly out of the ordinary about the behavior I am writing about. Anti-fatness is so pervasive in our society, and in our own thoughts, that even when I am recalling an encounter with a specific person, I do not feel that I am singling them out for critique; there is nothing singular about these individuals' actions or these stories. In our fatphobic world, most of the behavior I am reporting on here is seen as completely normal. We all have room for improvement.

Part of what made that song leader's quip so painful to me was the audience that he was speaking to: little kids who are already learning to judge their own bodies and other people's bodies as good or bad, desirable or undesirable, based on whether they are fat or thin. A synagogue preschool, of all places, should not be teaching these children that they need to police their enjoyment of holiday foods lest they turn into bodies that deserve derision. But here they were being taught that fat people cannot or should not dance, that no one would want to be in a body that could not dance, and that fat people would be left out of the dancing. This early exposure to anti-fat bias is a painful part of my own story, which I tell more expansively in chapter 1.

There are only so many aspects of human life that fat people can be excluded from before it becomes clear that fat people are being excluded from humanity itself. For this reason, confronting anti-fatness is a moral and even a theological issue. In Jewish tradition, we learn that every human being is created in the image of God. As I explore more in chapter 2, while fat people are consistently dehumanized, we too are imprinted with divinity.

The only thing that was refreshing about the blatant nature of the song leader's fat joke was that it did not pretend to care about fat people. Too often, anti-fatness is framed in terms of concerns for the health of fat people. The easiest way to tell that this concern is fake is that it does not feel like caring; caring, as I unpack further in chapter 3, is in the eye of the cared for.

Fat people deserve a spot on the dance floor—and in the classroom and at the family gathering—just as much as anyone else. One way of actually caring for the needs of fat folks is ensuring that our physical spaces are fat accessible. Chapter 4 looks at the issue of appropriate seating as one example of making space for fat people.

Unfortunately, we could turn every space into one in which fat people's physical needs are met while leaving intact the kind of speech that my daughter and I heard at her Chanukah party. While jokes about fat people abound, much of the anti-fat speech I encounter comes from people who are much thinner than I am talking about themselves and their fears of fatness. Chapter 5 delves into how we speak about our own bodies and their real or imagined fatness.

In addition to hurt and anger, the fat joke at the preschool Chanukah party also sparked another response in me: an upwelling of resistance, a deep knowing and desire to sing out a Torah of fat liberation. "Doesn't this guy know," I thought to myself, "that Chanukah celebrates the miracle of fat?!?"

Ready to rededicate the Temple after defeating the Syrian-Greek army, the Maccabees of the Chanukah story discovered that they only had enough oil to light the Temple's lamps for one day. The miracle of Chanukah is that that oil, that fat, lasted for eight days. We eat fried foods on Chanukah in remembrance of the luminous fat that allowed our traditions, and by extension our people, to survive. We celebrate fat as that which sustains and renews us in the face of hardship.

We also eat fried foods because fat is yummy. And we do not need to be afraid of or uncomfortable with our own fat hungers—neither the hunger of fat people nor the hunger for fat. All I wanted was for those kids to be able to enjoy their *sufganiyot* and their dancing in their own bodies of various sizes without anti-fatness interrupting them. Chapter 6 takes a cradle-to-grave look at what a truly loving embrace of fatness might look like.

Interspersed between each of the book's chapters are letters I have written but never sent. I offer them as deeper reflections on specific instances and impacts of anti-fatness in my own life. Like the longer chapters themselves, each one also illustrates the strength and joy to be found in learning and teaching a Torah that embraces fatness.

Central to the celebration of Chanukah is the *mitzvah* of "broadcasting the miracle." We are obligated to place the lights we light each night of the festival in such a way that they can be seen publicly. Fat acceptance—embracing fatness and resisting the anti-fat bias that I encounter every day—has illuminated my own life in innumerable ways. But, for far too long, I kept that light to myself. Here I am, ready both to shed light on the harm done by anti-fat bias and to deploy Jewish tradition itself as a bright beacon of justice and healing. May this book broadcast the miracle of fat liberation far and wide, sparking gleaming conversations among all who read it and spreading brilliant fat joy.

To my seven-year-old self

It is hard for me, as I write this, to distinguish what I want to say to you here from what I want to say to my own daughter, who is now your age and whose body looks much like yours. I want you both to know: your body is lovely not only the way it is right now but however it will grow to be. I would love you without condition no matter your size or shape, yet I also enjoy admiring your round little body's specific wonders, like how impressively strong you are. More than anything, I do not want you to diet.

At the same time, there are obvious differences between you two. My daughter is her own person, already so different from you, from me, in marvelous ways that I love learning more and more about. But here is a most important difference: I do not know her future, but I do know yours.

My sweet young self, I feel an oceanic connection with you across the vastness of time and space between us. I feel, I imagine, like Abram might have felt when he heard God's assurance (Genesis 15:13–14) that his great-grandchildren and their descendants would be enslaved for four hundred years and then they would be set free. Abram and I both see this journey of our loved ones' suffering and redemption from afar, powerless to alter its course. Yet Abram signs on to this covenant, taking the brokenness along with the promise, feeling in his own guts this future of wounding and healing, acknowledging how the prospect of belonging and homeland is stained with the tears of enslavement and the sweat of struggle.

You are about to get stuck in a place of narrow expectations of what your body ought to look like. You are about to spend half of your young life going round and round in this cycle: hating your body and feeling like the way you eat must be "out of control"; believing in yourself and your ability to make positive changes; feeling deep disappointment and confusion when dieting does not work; sliding back into self-hatred.

I feel unaccountably blessed that your years of dieting are now a hazy memory for me, a history almost as ancient as Abram's. At the same time, this history feels like an amulet that I carry with me, a holder of mystery, a protective talisman reminding me of that place of narrowness to which I hope never to return.

Unburying your story, holding it close like a sacred text, I find myself reading between the lines with newfound wonder: your body, your sweet little roundness, will do everything in its power to show how life yearns for more life. Far from being lazy, your body, your desire, your heart, your hunger will all work tirelessly to be heard and to grow. All of your "overeating" and "bingeing" and "sneaking" and "cheating," all of it, deep down, embodying your undying desire for freedom.

I know this for you especially when I focus on that part of the dieting cycle where you believe that something better than this stuckness must be possible. Everyone and everything around you is going to tell you that this hope must be conditioned on future "success" in making yourself shrink. They will tell you that freedom is what comes from turning your body into someone else's. But for just one moment, I want to catch you at that moment of pure yearning. Stick with this knowing that the way things are is not the way they ought to be! Let it be an angel accompanying you on this journey.

Until one day, I promise you—just as our ancestors in Egypt suffered silently for hundreds of years before beginning the crying out that would lead to their liberation—one day you will keep the hope but lose the dieting. One day enough will simply be enough.

And when you cry out for rescue, you will be answered abundantly, expansively. And like our enslaved ancestors, your diet-exhausted teenage body will somehow walk across the split sea on dry land, with a wall of water on one side and a wall of water on the other side. And you and I will dance together on the far shore and wiggle our toes in the sands of freedom.

1

From Narrowness to Freedom

I can still feel in my chest the rush of newfound freedom. I can still sense at my back the whoosh of an old, confining reality crumbling and being washed away like Pharaoh's army. I can still remember the thought that popped into my head that day: "On the other side of the wall, there is no wall." It was the beginning of my own journey to freedom. It was the day I decided to stop dieting. I was sixteen years old.

Every year, at the Passover seder table, Jewish tradition insists that we are meant to experience the Exodus from Egypt, *yetziat mitzrayim*, being freed from enslavement, "as if" each of us went through it ourselves. But since that day I stopped dieting, there has been no "as if" about this for me. There is a long tradition of translating *mitzrayim* as "the Narrow Places." I have been freed from the Narrow Places of dieting and hating my fat body, of buying into a truly narrow ideal of how human bodies ought to look, and of being a willing participant in my own oppression.

I want to tell you the story of this journey up to now. It is not a roadmap or any kind of prescription. But it is a story I rejoice in telling and retelling. And it is a path I rejoice in living. I have been stuck in narrowness and I have gotten out, and the journey is not over but there is no going back. Or, as my dear friend Elizabeth Tamny printed on buttons in the mid-1990s, "I'VE LET MYSELF GO . . . ASK ME HOW."[1]

Getting Stuck

Most of us who get stuck in narrowness get there for a reason. In Genesis, the journey into stuckness starts with a hunger. Like his father and grandfather before him, Jacob experiences a famine in the land of Canaan (Genesis 41:57). He sends his children to the Narrow Places to find nourishment, and their descendants end up enslaved in Egypt for generations.

My own journey into narrowness started innocently enough too. I was a smart, fat, Jewish seven-year-old going through a "famine" of not fitting in. My dieting was born of a hunger for friendship and belonging. If kids teased you because of what you looked like, little me reasoned, you should just change what you looked like. I wasn't interested in changing my smartness or my Jewishness, but my fatness? I yearned for a thinner me who had more friends. Everyone around me made weight loss seem like a very simple solution.

The instructions for my first diet were on a piece of legal-sized paper folded into a little booklet. They had been typed on a typewriter, mimeographed, and then passed on to me by a grown-up I trusted, a family friend. I remember the neat fractions and small numbers. For breakfast: half a grapefruit and one piece of toast or half a cup of oatmeal. The diet offered a version with 1,200 calories a day or, if you weren't as serious, an option for 1,600 calories a day. Of course, I was a good kid and only ever tried the 1,200 calorie version.

And when I say I "tried the 1,200 calorie version," I mean, of course, that I tried not once or twice but repeatedly, because (also of course) diets don't work. Dieting almost always means going from one diet to another, our weight going up and down and up again.

So I proceeded to try other diets and "food plans" and what today would be called "lifestyle changes" for the rest of my childhood. Like anyone would, with each "failure" I assumed the problem was that I was doing it wrong and that I just needed to keep trying until I found the one that I could do right.

Mentally, I was stuck in narrow expectations of what a body should look like, but I also felt stuck with a body that I could not narrow down. In retrospect, this lack of "success" was itself something of a blessing. I was, after all, meant to be growing. But there was so much sadness and fear around my growth. The sadness was my own, born of the belief that my body size meant that I did not belong. But the fear was all around me. I felt a deep sense of foreboding radiating from family members, teachers, and doctors. "Things might be alright now," they all seemed to say, "but everyone knows what this means for the future." I did not know what it meant for my future. And, of course, they did not actually know what it meant for my future either, but that didn't keep them from planting their worry in me.

Here is some of what I remember from that long decade of dieting.

I know that after I had gone back to the mimeographed booklet a few times, at some point I tried keeping a food diary. I remember reporting with deep shame, mixed with perhaps just a pinch of rebellion, that I had started out the week being "good" but then one day ate a whole sleeve of Thin Mints. Writing about it now, I feel a surge of love for my young body and its cellular unwillingness to give up its needs and desires.

There were also group dieting experiences, mostly, it seems, in church buildings. There was WeightWatchers, with its dreaded public weigh-ins in the church basement. And there were the special Weight-Watchers foods you could buy in the grocery store. They had these "desserts" that came frozen in a shallow square paper bowl. You were supposed to defrost them slightly in the microwave, but when I ate one that was still partly frozen, I imagined it must have tasted better when it was fully defrosted, and when I ate one that was fully defrosted I imagined it must have tasted better if it was still frozen. And I remember low-cal "milkshakes" that were made in a blender with a packet of powder and lots and lots of ice. They tasted like chalk and air; perhaps those were their two main ingredients. Sometimes I ate diet bread— each bite revealing its close family connection to a kitchen sponge.

And there was Overeaters Anonymous (OA), this one in the upstairs of a church. I don't claim to know what OA is like now, but my group was definitely nothing but a spiritually tinged dieting support group. Most of what I remember, in addition to being the only kid there, is that a big deal was often made of the fact that we were not a GreySheet group. I had no idea what a GreySheet group was—I still don't—but it sounded like a cult. Looking back, I wonder if this was emphasized mostly so that we could claim that our own devotion to restricting our eating was *not* a cult. Of course, there was also more than a little admiration expressed for those strict Grey-Sheeters, whoever they were.

One thing I learned at OA was that thin, tall, long-straight-dark-haired beautiful flight attendants could also feel terrible about their bodies and the ways they ate. This was actually an important thing to learn. I also surmised that this particular flight attendant's disordered eating was, to my preteen judgmental thinking anyway, way more "messed up" than my eating. At one evening's meeting, she told a story about how she snuck a cookie off of a passenger's dinner tray and how then she had to eat the cookies off of every single dinner tray in the galley so that no one would know. And my little preadolescent brain thought, "But you're so skinny, why do *you* hate your body?"

I felt sorry for her and also somehow superior to her: my dislike of my body was loudly affirmed by society at large, but hers seemed like it was clearly something gone awry internally. In retrospect, she and I were "sneaking" food for exactly the same reason: people in authority were trying to control our eating and our body size. This was before unions fought to force airlines to begin loosening weight restrictions for flight attendants in the early 1990s. Her job depended on her maintaining a certain low weight. I know her body made her miserable, but I wish I could go back and give that body a huge hug. She wasn't just eating all the cookies; she was stealing them from her fatphobic corporate employers!

Restricting what I ate naturally led to "overeating," which I am defining here simply as eating more than everyone thought I was supposed to eat. The whole time I was dieting as a child, I was also, alternately, "overeating." And because I had absorbed the message that eating what I wanted to eat was by definition "bad," it meant that I too was sneaking food. I never ate all the cookies from all the dining service trays on an airplane, but I furtively ate a lot of bowls of

Cracklin' Oat Bran cereal at babysitting gigs after my charges were asleep. Foods like Cracklin' Oat Bran, and other "sugar cereals," were never allowed in my house. One particularly memorable secret eating event while babysitting involved accidentally biting heartily into a big hunk of unsweetened baker's chocolate. To this day I can conjure up the bitter taste of my mistake.

I stole money from my mother's wallet to buy candy and other "forbidden" foods. I hid M&Ms in my pockets and stealthily, or so I thought, ate them while watching TV with my family.

My friend D and I bought Hostess pies and other plasticky baked goods at the corner store next to her house and ate them together. The chocolatey coating was so unappealing, and yet I licked and peeled and picked off every bit where it stuck to its cellophane packaging. D and I would sneak into the playground behind the Catholic school. Doing drugs? Smoking cigarettes? Making out? No, we were just eating together in secret.

My young body was also subjected to a more "scientific" approach to figuring out what I supposedly should and should not eat. I underwent "food allergy" blood tests and a glucose tolerance test meant to prove "scientifically" that I was eating the wrong way.

This scientifically suspect testing yielded a long and baffling list of foods I was no longer allowed to eat. In the ensuing months, I ate a lot of lamb and butter and a particular tuna rice salad that I can still taste. I proudly made it for myself as a twelve-year-old: brown rice, canned tuna, sliced black olives, grated carrots, chopped parsley, and Paul Newman's Own salad dressing. Even at family meals, I ate different food than the rest of my family. I remember eating little lamb chops that were stuffed with ground lamb. I ate a lot of almonds. Rice cakes with almond butter. Rice cakes with real butter. No sugar, no eggs, no chicken, no beef. Nectarines yes, but peaches no. I was allowed to eat butter and heavy cream, but not other milk products. A real "treat" was bananas and heavy cream, with a sprinkling of fructose powder on top. No to wheat; yes to oats.

Obviously, some people have actual allergies or sensitivities to certain foods, others have real diseases that can be managed through diet, and still others without specific diagnoses experience relief of various symptoms when they refrain from eating particular things. None of these were the case for me. I was doing it because I was promised that I would lose weight if I ate this way. I did not lose weight.

There is a dreamlike quality to all of this. How long did each diet last? How much of a break did I get between diets or "food plans"? The diets came and went, but the hatred of my body never stopped. Wondering what was wrong with me was a constant. How could I achieve all kinds of things in school but not lose weight? How could such a smart and hardworking girl be so "stupid" and "lazy" about this?

My body's refusal to comply with my wishes made me hate myself more. My whole sense of my worth as a human being rose and fell in inverse relationship to the numbers on the scale. None of my successes in other arenas were ever enough to counteract my sense of failure at not being able to control my size. So much of my energy and my thought and my time went into hating my body and wishing it was different than it was. I had swallowed whole our culture's contempt for fat people, and in so doing, I had unwittingly signed on to be the primary taskmaster in my own enslavement.

Getting Unstuck

When I first stopped dieting, I still hoped I could lose weight. Already in the mid-1980s, a few books promised as much, like Geneen Roth's

Feeding the Hungry Heart[2] and *Breaking Free from Compulsive Eating*[3] and Jane Hirschmann and Carol Munter's *Overcoming Overeating*.[4] The anti-fat premise of these approaches, which was also shared in early editions of Evelyn Tribole and Elyse Resch's *Intuitive Eating*,[5] was essentially that fatness was caused by the inevitable cycle of dieting and bingeing and that if you stopped dieting you would automatically reach your—always thinner—"natural weight." I read most of those books as a teenager and even attended workshops with some of the authors.

I now view these books as kind of a gateway drug to freedom. Even though at first I still pinned my hopes on their promises of being thinner, once I had stopped dieting and stopped weighing myself all the time, I was ready to start learning about fat acceptance. I cannot overemphasize the importance of this *stopping*. It was a loud and clear "no!" to the forces of narrowness. Even before I had grasped onto anything new, I was letting go of what clearly was not working.

The repeated refrain of Exodus is "Let My people go, that they may serve Me." The letting go, the "no," comes first. This is freedom *from* before we can get to any kind of freedom *to*. And there is a surety and a certainty to this "no!" that the more amorphous "yes" can lack.

Freed from dieting, I had no idea what would come next. I had no plan for how to eat, how to be in my body, or even how to live once I gave up on all my plans for weight loss. Like my ancestors before me, I did not leave the Narrow Places because I knew the way to a promised land. I left because I could no longer stay. And like my ancestors before me, I doubt if I would have made it out alone.

That I found my way to the fat acceptance movement in those pre-internet days feels like nothing short of a miracle. Print publications sent via snail mail were like little stepping stones on my journey. First I found *Radiance: The Magazine for Large Women*, and then somehow that led me to homemade zines like Marilyn Wann's *FAT!SO?*, Hanne Blank Boyd's *Zaftig*, and the Fat Girl Collective's *FaT GiRL: a zine for fat dykes and the women who want them*. It must have been through *Radiance* that I initially found out about the National Association to Advance Fat Acceptance (NAAFA).

Founded in 1969, NAAFA remains the longest-running organization promoting equality for everyone regardless of size. I joined in my late teens in the early 1990s and began attending fat feminist gatherings and local NAAFA meet-ups. It was through these connections that I found a community that offered me education, friendship, and my first glimpses of fat joy.

I came back from those gatherings with T-shirts that said things like "Women of Substance, Women of Power" and "FLAB: Fat Lesbian Action Brigade." Wearing these T-shirts was one bold way of my own coming out as fat. Indeed, "coming out as fat" is itself not a bad translation of *yetziat mitzrayim*—emerging from narrowness. My own coming out as fat was absolutely facilitated by the fat lesbian feminists at whose feet I was learning. They were my elders—as a teenager this could have meant they were any age above thirty—and many of them had already been involved in organized fat activism for its first two decades.

While it was largely not oriented toward fat liberation in the least, the gay liberation movement of the late 1980s and early 1990s was also an important inspiration to me. My tiny liberal arts college did not have any other fat activists on campus, as far as I could tell, but the growing outspokenness of my gay classmates was vital to my understanding of what it meant to live beyond narrow societal expectations of who we were meant to be.

I remember walking with a group of friends through a part of campus we called "Siberia" and talking about the nicknames we had had in high school. One in our group hadn't spoken yet, so someone asked him, "What about you, R, what was your nickname in high school?" To which R flatly answered, "Faggot." A brief moment of silence was followed by the liberatory laughter of people appreciative of the relatively fresh freedom of loving themselves and one another as they are.

This was in the late 1980s, before there was any effective treatment for HIV/AIDS, when SILENCE=DEATH was *the* slogan of AIDS activism and if you cared at all about gay liberation, you would walk around proudly wearing buttons that said things like "a tisket, a tasket, a condom or a casket." I have a strong memory of one group of "grown-up" Black gay activists who came to our college to give a presentation and strode around campus looking buff and handsome. They wore tight white T-shirts with words printed in huge black letters on the front. One said "GAY LIBERATION," while another said simply "ANAL SEX." The boldness of this great proud "no!" to being fearfully closeted was indispensable to my own burgeoning sense of how a person could be themselves in public.

Another schoolmate read Jim Everhard's poem "Curing Homosexuality" at an open mic night with its unforgettable lines "Hatred is always self-hatred. / Denial is always fear." The poem ends with the lines:

None of us knows how he got here,
for what reason we are here or
why we are who we are.
It is not obvious
and a swish doesn't make me any more obvious
than the lack of one.
I am obvious

I bear such a debt of gratitude to gay liberation and to the young people around me on my college campus who were sharing their own coming-out journeys with us all. In my fatness, I was obvious too. And I was burning with rage at a world that told me not to be. How could I not be enraged? As Ani DiFranco sang:

If you're not angry
you're just stupid

or you don't care
how else can you react
when you know
something's so unfair

My anger was so important to this part of my journey. I needed that constant, giant "fuck you!" to the fatphobic world to get the self-hatred out of me. As angry as I had been at myself for not being able to lose weight, I was now—much more healthily—directing my anger at anyone or anything that suggested there was a problem with my size.

I was not going to diet. I was not going to put up with anyone placing any moral value on anything I ate. I was also not going to wear a bra or shave any body hair because "fuck you and your fascist beauty standards!"

There was so much to be angry about, and there still is. In addition to the discrimination that fat people as a group face in employment and education and on and on, anti-fat bias deeply impacted me in personal ways. For years after I stopped dieting, my father would try to gently have conversations with me about how he was worried that because of my size I would "end up alone." He definitely got a healthy dose of "fuck you!" in reply. When anyone around me expressed their own desire to lose weight, I could hear it only as a personal attack on my own body that warranted a counterattack. And straight boys as a whole group evoked in me song lyrics about their inexcusable failure to "see the goddess that is me."

I raged for the better part of a decade, becoming involved in all kinds of fights against injustice that seemed just as unfair as anti-fatness. I wrote a master's thesis on lesbian invisibility in healthcare; I sang at protests to close down the School of the Americas at Fort Benning; I wrote songs condemning the US sanctions against Saddam Hussein's Iraq; once, if memory serves, I even demonstrated against the General Assembly of the Jewish Federations of North America, though I do not remember why.

Over and over again our tradition commands us to "love the stranger," explaining that we are not to oppress the stranger "for you know the soul of the stranger, for you were strangers in the land of Egypt" (Exodus 23:9). My own experience of being othered as a fat woman, my own history of being stuck in narrowness, stoked my bone-deep fire to fight against all forms of oppression and marginalization. While I was deeply grateful to be free of dieting, I was also spurred on by Fannie Lou Hamer's reminder that "nobody is free until everybody's free."

At one fat women's gathering, the keynote was delivered by Carol Munter. She had written *Overcoming Overeating*, with its implied promise of weight loss, but her work too had evolved, and by 1995 she and coauthor Jane Hirschmann had written *When Women Stop Hating Their Bodies*.[6] "Imagine the energy that could be unleashed," Munter invited us in her speech, "if women stopped body shaping and started world shaping." I was definitely unleashed.

Theologically, this wrathful approach to justice imagines a God in its own image: a God who swiftly judges and punishes wrongdoing. In the Jewish mystical tradition, this version of God aligns with the divine attribute of *Gevurah* (Might) or *Din* (Judgment). This is the aspect of God that sets hard boundaries, knows no mercy, and would destroy the world with fiery fury rather than put up with injustice. Looking back, I cannot imagine how I could have started on my path of liberation without such a big dose of this vengeful approach to righting the world's wrongs. I was one proud fat woman against a world of stigma and bias, and my wrath was my own "pillar of fire" (Exodus 13:21) guiding me through oppression's darkest night.

Freed to Wander

But then something started to shift in me. For one thing, I started to be disturbed by how my anger got in the way of seeing my "enemies" as human beings. At one protest to "Free East Timor" outside the Indonesian consulate in Chicago, I had been singing into the megaphone. The cops had arrived to break up our protest, and since none of us were planning on getting arrested that day, we slowly started to disperse. Among the cops asking us to move along, one Chicago police officer who looked to be in his sixties motioned me over. I approached him cautiously, expecting some kind of reprimand. And he did shout at me, but it was not what I had anticipated: "You ever hear of Kate Smith? Because you really remind me of her. What a voice she had!" Here was the embodiment of "them" in my clear us/them mindset, and he was comparing me to a fat singing icon and shout-suggesting, "Y'know what? You oughta sing at Cubs games."

His fellow cops tried to get him back to the stern disbursement they were supposed to be enacting, while my fellow protesters kept looking over at me to make sure I was okay. In fact, I was both bemused and a bit shaken by his effusive praise. It touched my heart, and I felt like I was not allowed to have my heart touched by a cop at a protest. It shook up the binary thinking that my wrath usually held in place. The clarity my wrath provided, of a world where everything and everyone was either on our side of good or on their side of evil, was clouded by the tears this cop's heartfelt compliment brought to my eyes.

It was the opposite of a radicalizing moment. My politics—my sense of what was wrong with the world and how it had gotten that way—did not change significantly, but I was starting to be less and less sure of what the best strategies were for change making. I still believed in the power of less body shaping, more world shaping. My commitment to *tikkun olam* was as strong as ever, but I was no longer clear on how best to actualize my commitment to healing the world. What was my work in this life? What was my part to play?

I was also beginning to wonder whether raging for justice was really good for my own mental well-being. I had reached a crisis point where I was caught, as we all are, in the chasm between what

I had and what I wanted, the world as it is and the world as I wished it could be. And I was burned out on trying to get what I wanted, on fighting for a better world, both personally—especially in the form of a series of unrequited crushes—and in my activism work. I was tired of the us/them polarization. I was tired of my own certainties and self-righteousness. I was tired of feeling like mostly I was getting off on my own anger. The fire of my rage was mostly feeding back on itself and stoking more and more rage.

Seeds of doubt were sprouting about whether anger was really the way toward lasting change. My wrath had been invaluable in securing my freedom from the narrowness of dieting and hating my body. But its unwavering judgmental "no!" was wearing on me, and I needed to step back from the megaphone, at least for the time being.

In the course of one memorable week at the end of the 1990s, I managed to find a new therapist, explore taking a yoga class, and start meditating for the first time. I had been becoming more involved in my synagogue and in Jewish spiritual practice, and I wanted to learn Jewish meditation. At the time, I could not find any such thing in Chicago, and so, like many Jews before me and since, I fell in with some lovely Buddhists.

Since I could not *have* what I *wanted*, I really hoped that meditation would teach me to *want* what I already *had*, to be blissfully at peace with the world as it is. Instead, meditation was teaching me to truly want what I want, to gratefully have what I have, and to be able, at least in moments, to sit in the silence of the vast wilderness between those two. Leaving Egypt, so many of us expect a quick trip to the Promised Land. But like those ancient Israelites, I was instead freed to wander in a desert of uncertainty.

Wandering in the desert, the people of Israel complain about missing the familiar aspects of their former life of slavery. They miss the certainty of always having "the cucumbers, the melons, the leeks, the onions, and the garlic" (Numbers 11:5). When I was stuck in the narrows of dieting and hating my body, I was repeatedly assured of certainties in life—being thin was better than being fat; eat less and exercise more and you will lose weight; try harder and you will succeed—as if the ideal body is a bomb calorimeter, a controlled experiment. My wrathful approach to fat liberation had also offered certainties: I am right and you are wrong; fatness has absolutely nothing to do with health ever; "if you're not angry then you're just stupid or you don't care." There is a deep comfort in these certainties. They can help us fend off many fears—fears of loneliness, illness, and ultimately death. Living in genuine freedom is painful; it offers no promise that if you follow this plan you will be saved from pain or loss. A human body *can* be healthy, or at least temporarily disease free, at any size; one can also be sick at any size. Fat people absolutely face bias in the dating world, but making good matches for people of all sizes remains as daunting and miraculous as splitting the Red Sea (BT Sotah 2a).

Amid the uncertainty, I was still deeply grateful as I saw my theology, which had centered the God of Powerful Justice (*Gevurah/Din*), now make room for the bountiful flow of *Ḥesed* (lovingkindness). I was willing to give up the "pillar of fire" that had been my guide for the softer, if more amorphous, "pillar of cloud" (Exodus 13:21). The more I sat in meditation, the more this understanding deepened: it makes sense that NAAFA chose the term "fat acceptance," yes *acceptance*, because this is actually about being with what is. Setting aside my T-shirts with their bold slogans, now my activism became much more about simply showing up in my own body without apologizing for it.

Slowly my relationship with my body shifted again, particularly in how I dealt with either real or imagined fatphobia coming at me.

My go-to response to attacks on my choices about dieting and my body had been to scream, at least internally, "I don't have to defend myself to YOU!" This is, of course, an extremely defensive thing to scream. And I noticed this tendency yielding to a more accepting and gentler stance until one day, mid-meditation, this thought arose: "There is nothing here that needs defending." My anger had saved my life; now something quieter and less fiery was saving my sanity and my soul.

I am distrustful of the idea that we can move right from hating our bodies to loving them. For me, truly loving my body is something that arises in passing moments when I practice a more neutral willingness to be with what is. After many months on this new leg of my journey from narrowness to freedom, with "acceptance" as my new watchword, I was walking along one day and suddenly felt an upwelling of tenderness for my own shadow, the shape of my fat body stretching out there on the sidewalk in front of me with the sun at my back.

I tried to practice acceptance of others as well. I knew that dieting was not good for me, but I was not quite as willing, verbally at least, to condemn others who might think it was good for them. Who was I to know what was right for other people? On a pragmatic level, this openness and attempt to be accepting of everything as it is served me well in attending a pluralistic rabbinical school and working in synagogues where I certainly would not have lasted long if I constantly gave fiery sermons on fat liberation from the pulpit.

This gentler path also allowed me to be open to trying new things. I had been getting more involved in Jewish observance, but up until this point, I had always been resistant to the idea of *kashrut*, not sure how I could engage with any practice around food without my old self-judgment returning. Then one day I decided that I wanted to be able to make a blessing before eating each meal. I could not imagine what a blessing over a cheeseburger or a ham sandwich might be. I am not by any means suggesting that there are no such blessings, just that for me I was drawing a blank about what they might be. I decided to give keeping kosher a try as an expression of my love for God and for Jewish tradition. Again, I want to be clear that my story here is descriptive of my own journey and not prescriptive of what anyone else's journey should be. I do not think that keeping kosher makes me a "better Jew," much less a better human being, than anyone else or even that it makes me better than my past non-kosher-keeping self.

I was aware at each step of the way that my angrier self would see many of these changes as selling out, choosing conformity, or sliding down a slippery slope of assimilation back into narrowness. However, another difference in this new phase of my journey was that I was learning to live from the inside out: focusing on experiencing the body through living out into the world through my senses rather than living by imagining what my body or my choices looked like from the outside. I was no longer willing to make decisions based on how they might fit or not fit into a narrowly conceived political framework.

"Living from the inside out" could be another translation of *yetziat mitzrayim*, an alternative interpretation of Exodus from Narrow Places: continually letting ourselves go by living outward from within the narrowness of any individual body as it sits in its place in the vastness of the universe.

Singing up the Well

In the decades since I began shifting from rage to acceptance, or at least trying to, I have never lost my own knowing that anti-fatness is deeply wrong. I was certainly still sharing this view with those who were closest to me or who asked for my thoughts on intentional weight loss. I have also never had a shortage of opportunities to be vocal about how I relate to my own body, especially since, no matter how nonconfrontational I ever imagined myself to be, others—from strangers on the street, to new friends, to nearly every medical professional ever—have never stopped confronting me with their fatphobic opinions, intrusive queries, and unsolicited advice.

I also knew that showing up in my own body and not apologizing for it is indeed a powerful form of activism. I do not doubt that my own embrace of fatness rippled through a number of both passing and longer-lasting connections I made with others, offering an example of a more loving way to be in the body. When it came to the connection between individual liberation and collective liberation, I trusted that this quieter approach to activism still had some wider impact.

But one preschool Chanukah party with a fatphobic song leader changed all that. I was no longer satisfied with silence. It was time to sing out, time to use my big voice, the voice of "no!" and the voice of "yes!" It was time to "lift your voice like a shofar" (Isaiah 58:1) against the injustice of anti-fatness. It was time to launch Fat Torah, not only as my own quiet approach to being a fat rabbi and writing a blog post about it here and there, but as something I was ready to share and grow in the world. It was time to write this book.

Some have said that this must surely be a consequence of parenthood, and there may be some truth in that. It is one thing for me as a grown individual to hold my peace in public while anti-fat tropes, architectures, and policies—both written and unwritten—rule the day. It is something else entirely to let my children grow up in such a world without hearing their mother speak out against it loudly. Go on and on about your diet and how "bad" you have been, and I can decide whether to intervene or to just accept you for who you are, where you are. But I am less willing to let that same anti-fat rhetoric go unchallenged when I know the harm it does to those I love.

If not the wrathful pillar of fire or the it's-all-good pillar of cloud, then what guides me now on this winding path from narrowness to freedom? Three times in Deuteronomy, and then echoing through Psalms, and in the Passover Hagaddah, we hear that God took us out of the Narrow Places "with a strong hand and an outstretched arm." Doublings or pairs like this in our sacred texts are always opportunities for rich interpretation. Looking back on my journey up to now and inviting others to join me on the way forward, I imagine the strong hand and the outstretched arm as the pairing of anger and acceptance, their coupling necessary for the kind of activist I aspire to be now.

Jewish mystics see *Gevurah/Din* (powerful judgment) and *Ḥesed* (lovingkindness) as two arms of a single divine body. The Zohar, a central Jewish mystical text, reads a verse from the biblical Song of Songs (2:6) as showing how judgment and love complement, balance, and strengthen one another: "His left hand is under my head, and his right hand embraces me." Rage or acceptance, by themselves, will not get the job done. Instead, divine fruitfulness and true freedom flow from the coming together, the harmonizing, the dance of righteous anger and unbounded love.

Yet we need more than just wrath and compassion. We need curiosity and humor, joy and grief. We need to call on all of our available parts to be God's partners in the ongoing work of world shaping. "Turn it and turn it for everything is in it," Ben Bag Bag says of Torah (Pirkei Avot 5:22). The same could be said of the selves we bring to change making. Our own everything—our own whole selves—is what we take on this quest.

I feel these many forces dancing in me as I recommit to letting the joy of my own freedom from narrowness strengthen my renewed louder call for an embrace of all bodies. We learn, in a variety of *midrashim*, or interpretive teachings, that when we experience a miraculous rescue, we are meant to offer God songs of thanksgiving. The paradigmatic song in this tradition is the biblical "Song of the Sea" that Moses and the Children of Israel sing on the shores of the sea on their way out of the Narrow Places. Teaching a Torah that embraces fatness is my own way of singing a song of gratitude for having been rescued from narrowness.

The "Song of the Sea" actually has two versions in the book of Exodus: the more expansive song of Moses and the people is immediately followed by an invitation from Moses's sister Miriam for all the women to dance and drum with her while she sings her own song. At first glance, the two songs have similar first lines, but a key difference was pointed out to me by Rabbi Sharon Cohen Anisfeld in the blessing she offered me when I was ordained as a rabbi. Moses sings, "*I will sing* to YHVH for He has triumphed!" (Exodus 15:1). Moses's song is in the first-person singular. By contrast, Miriam offers a song that exhorts those around her to join her with their own voices: "*Sing* to YHVH for He has triumphed!" (Exodus 15:21).

It is a wonderful thing to lift up our individual voice, rejoicing in our own freedom. But my aim is to strive to be more like Miriam: using my voice to bring others into song. My hope is that opening my mouth in sharing my fat freedom song—my own journey toward a world that embraces fatness—will encourage others to lift their voices as well.

We have, of course, a long way to go to birth a fat-embracing world. But here, too, I find Torah giving me strength for the journey. Reading the narrative of the Children of Israel crossing the Sea of Reeds on their way to freedom in Exodus, it looks as if both Moses's and Miriam's songs were sung when everyone had safely reached the other side. However, a powerful interpretation—by Sforno, a sixteenth-century Italian commentator—imagines that the people began their thanksgiving song not from a place of safety but in the very moments when they were walking across the sea with a wall of water on one side, a wall of water on the other side, and the horses and chariots of Pharoah's army galloping up behind them. We need to be able to imagine our own abundant collective freedom while the world is still in the narrowest of straits. We need to believe with the psalmist, who sings, "When I cried out to Yah from the Narrows, Yah answered me with expansiveness" (Psalm 118:5).

We can allow the dreamed-for expanse of our fat joy to power us forward on our journey. I envision this as a practice of "singing up the well." Throughout their trek from liberation to the Promised Land, according to Talmud (BT Taanit 9a), the Children of Israel were followed by a well of water. The well had been with them through the merit of Miriam, and once she died, the people had to learn how to "sing up the well" for themselves. "Arise, O well, sing to it!" was their song (Numbers 21:17).

I am not alone on this long, and nonlinear, journey from the first taste of my own body freedom to the promised land of liberation for all bodies. One of my deepest joys since founding Fat Torah has been connecting with others who yearn for their own freedom and for a fat-embracing world. Together, we can practice singing up a well that lets the living waters of our own liberation quench our thirst enough to keep us going on the way to that land flowing with milk and honey for all.

To my doctor who was proud of me for not having gestational diabetes

I was reminded of you today when my kickboxing teacher told me that she was proud of me and hoped I felt proud of myself. I've been learning with her for the last several months, and until now, it had been all boxing and no kicking. But today she decided that I was ready to learn a front kick. It was challenging to get the form right, but it felt really good. My punches and kicks don't look like hers, but I trust her enough to believe her when she says that I'm doing something right.

    I trusted you too. I put my pregnancy, my baby, my body in your hands. And you were one of the best doctors I have ever had. You spend a lot of time with your patients. This was a challenge during the hours of waiting in the hallway, watching my day slip away, while you gave other people your undivided attention. But once it was me in the room with you, all was forgiven.

My trust in you was built by your calm manner, your willingness to explain things to me, and your clarity that the many choices to be made in medical treatment during pregnancy were ultimately mine to make. You wanted me to be screened early for gestational diabetes, because my age and my size were risk factors. I didn't want to do the test you were sending me for. It's nauseating and time-consuming, and it is usually only done once folks "fail" an initial, less nauseating and time-consuming screening. But I try to pick my battles, and this did not seem worth arguing about.

When the test showed that I did not have gestational diabetes, you seemed almost startled. "Wow! I'm so proud of you!" you exclaimed. And then you just kept gushing, "I can tell that you're really making such an effort!"

But I wasn't making any kind of effort. I was continuing, as I had before my pregnancy, to try to eat whatever I wanted to eat and to move however I felt like moving. You never asked about the nature of my effort, and with your every "compliment," I could feel my individuality fading away a bit more behind layers and layers of expectations, assumptions, and judgments.

I know you need to see me and each of your patients as cases that can be categorized, plotted on graphs of chances of the many different things that can go wrong, large and small. Meanwhile, my humanity becomes hazy under all these generalizations. Some of them, I understand, are necessary for doing your job, but all of them can also be damaging to a patient's personhood. What matters most about me as a singular human has nothing to do with my body's reaction to drinking a sugary drink or any actions or inactions on my part that could supposedly have caused my body to react in one way or another. Mostly what I learned from your crowing on my behalf was that its opposite is almost surely true: you believe that your fat patients who do have gestational diabetes are categorically to blame for how their bodies handle sugar; you assume that they must not be trying hard enough. You made me frightened of your future decrees should my body ever yield test results that you were not so proud of.

When my kickboxing teacher says that she's proud of me, she is peeling away the veils of assumption and expectation. She is assessing me based on whatever intention she and I have set together and the visible effort that I put into moving toward that goal, whether I actually reach it this time or not. When she's proud of me, she brings more and more of my unique inner spark into the world. When you praised me for not having gestational diabetes—for being an anomaly in your sea of prejudgments—you obscured that spark.

2

Fatness and the Divine Image

Jewish tradition has so many juicy things to teach about what it means to be a human being. I could start this chapter with anything from a verse from an ancient text, to a medieval interpretive take, to a moving anecdote. Instead, in trying to write about what fatness and humanity have to do with one another, I find myself oscillating between sadness, disbelief, and rage. Why? Because the only reason this chapter needs to exist is because of how hard we fat folks have to fight to demonstrate that we are, in fact, human beings. Even as I write it, I can hardly believe that the central message of this chapter is "fat people are people."

Yet I do find solace for my raging heart in Torah, as well as strength for the ongoing fight. In fact, when a recent social media post by a prominent fat activist asked people to list their favorite fat liberation texts, I responded, perhaps somewhat cheekily, "Genesis 1:27." It is in this verse, right in Torah's opening chapter, that we hear how "God created humankind . . . in the image of the Divine" (*b'tzelem Elohim*). From these deepest mythic roots flows the assurance of our birthright: every single one of us is of immeasurable, unconditional worth; each of us is unique; our humanity is not something we have to earn; we are called to be partners with God in the ongoing work of creation; and we are all deserving of basic respect and care.[1]

Immeasurable Worth

In the somewhat startling context of instructions for preparing the witnesses in a death penalty case, Mishnah Sanhedrin (4:5) teaches that being created *b'tzelem Elohim* means that every human being is of infinite worth: "Anyone who destroys one person . . . it is as if they destroy a whole world. And anyone who sustains one person . . . it is as if they sustain a whole world."

Flowing from the Infinite, our worth is immeasurable. This can be shocking to contemplate and hard to take in for so many of us

Every Body Beloved | 57

who have been taught that our worth fluctuates based on the numbers on the scale: increasing in value and esteem if the numbers go down and, almost inevitably, decreasing when the numbers go up again. And this is not only a problem of how we value ourselves. The wage gap between fat people and our thin counterparts also suggests that our time and our labor are less valuable.[2] In most social contexts, our attractiveness or desirability is also "scored" as lower. In school settings, we literally receive lower grades for the same work.[3]

This kind of measuring gets particularly complicated when it comes to measurements of health.[4] We do not even need to wade into arguments here about whether weight itself is an accurate or useful measure of health. Even the most reliable tests of particular health measures are too often used in ways that convey an assessment not only of our health but of our human worth. This is a place where anti-fatness and ableism intersect: We are made to feel that we ourselves are failures if a blood test comes back outside of the normal range, and we can feel a strange sense of pride when we "pass" a given test.

Fat people who are privileged with "praiseworthy" health measures can also fall into the trap of "playing the good fatty," a term coined by fat activist Stacy Bias. More than once, when a doctor has suggested some kind of weight-loss intervention that I knew was not a good idea for me, I have tried to use any "good" lab test results I might have to prove my worthiness and to defend myself from their bias. This is a completely understandable tactic in the unlevel playing field of the doctor's office. But in the long run, it reinforces the idea that fat people are blameworthy when our test results are "bad."

Our value as human beings is not conditional on our health. And even the most accurate medical tests are meant to measure how much of what kind of care we might need, not whether we are trying hard enough to merit competent medical treatment.

Every Fat Person Is Unique

While we are completely equal in terms of our infinite, immeasurable worth, each fat person, like every human being, is also completely unique. Our text in Mishnah Sanhedrin (4:5) expresses this through a *midrash* (interpretive teaching) about the stamping of coins. If a person, a human king, for example, engraves coins with his image, every single coin looks the same. But God imprints each of us human beings with the likeness of the original human, created in God's own image, and each of us looks different. The diversity of human form is meant to be celebrated as a mark of God's greatness.

Meanwhile, fat people, too often, face the dehumanization of having our uniqueness go unseen. We are stereotyped, made invisible, or portrayed in dehumanizing ways in the media and forced to deal with people who cannot seem to tell one fat person from another.

Stereotypes flatten out each person's individuality. I am not going to give too much ink here to describing the stereotypes of fat people and fatness. But I will say that fat people should be allowed to be funny and joyous without worrying about being pigeonholed as jolly. We are allowed to be smart without constantly feeling pressure to prove that we are not stupid. We are allowed to be warm without getting stuck in ideas about fat people being effusively, if asexually, affectionate. And, God knows, we should be allowed to eat in public without people constantly making assumptions, and too frequently comments as well, about what we are eating and what it signifies to the observer about whether we are behaving "appropriately" for a person of our size. In other words, I should be able to eat a salad, if I feel like it, without people complimenting me for "being good." And I should be able to eat dessert without anyone shaming me or, more frequently, trying to publicly commiserate with me about "being bad."

When it comes to representations of fat people in the media, we are woefully underrepresented in all but the most stereotyped roles. More often we are simply invisible. This is quite the irony, considering that we are also seen as an overwhelming looming menace, taking up way too much space with bodies that are viewed as inherently diseased. So we are, if you will, invisible in plain sight.

When fat people are part of a news story, we are often "headless fatties," fat activist Charlotte Cooper's term for the ubiquitous stock photos and B-roll depicting fat bodies only from the neck down or with our faces obscured. These sweet, uniquely varied faces that make us each human, literally erased.

All of this anti-fatness is, of course, also easily internalized, which can impact our own sense of where and how we are "allowed" to show up. One Jewish educator, who was doing some supervision with me around bringing more fat liberation into the classroom, reported imagining what it would be like to wear a bathing suit at the beach. He pictured himself without his usual shirt to cover up his round belly and then had this thought arise in his head: "No one wants to look at *that*!" It was such a painful and true encapsulation of the highly visible invisibility of fat people, the ways we are othered, and the ways we other ourselves. If you recoil at the very thought of seeing fat bodies, it is not surprising that you would be more comfortable not including us in your picture of humanity.

Our uniqueness is also diminished when you confuse one fat person for another. More than one professor would often mix up my name with that of a rabbinical school classmate or would think they had had a conversation with me that they had actually had with her, or vice versa. My classmate and I love each other deeply, but beyond our fatness—and our bodies are not even the same size or shape—we are really quite different human beings.

I recently experienced a similar manifestation of this inability to truly see the diversity of fat bodies, and each one's uniqueness, when I showed a visiting rabbinical student around my Jerusalem neighborhood. I was delighted to know that a fellow fat liberationist would be living close by, if only for a brief time, and I was also looking forward to getting to know her better. So imagine my mortification when I excitedly introduced her to a neighbor we ran into, only to have him interrupt my introduction to say, "Oh, this is your sister?" Beyond our fatness and our hair color, we do not particularly resemble one another.

By contrast, paying loving—or at least neutral—attention to fat bodies, learning to see and celebrate fat body diversity, is a joyous pursuit. I fondly remember my own astonishment at the first fat women's gatherings I attended in my late teens and early twenties. I was used to being the fattest person in the room, one of the only people of my size in most social settings. Yet I found myself not only relishing what it felt like to be with people who were "like me" but also enjoying all the many ways our bodies were actually so different from one another. I was happy to spend hours, right there in a hotel conference room in Parsippany, New Jersey, gazing around me at bodies of different shapes, sizes, skin tones, and gender expressions, each with its own unique proportions, rolls, and roundnesses—these many geographies embodying the Mishnah's insistence that each of us is an entire world.

You Do Not Have to Be Good

As the first COVID-19 vaccines were being rolled out, fatness was believed to be a risk factor for worse outcomes from the virus. Because of this, those of us in larger bodies above a certain body mass index (BMI) were given priority in being vaccinated. I was excited about the possibility of being vaccinated and said so in an online community devoted to evidence-based medicine. In response, a straight-sized group member wrote that it was unfair that my BMI made me eligible to be vaccinated before she was because my size was, in her words, "a lifestyle choice."

Fat people are fat for many different reasons. Many different factors go into any human being's size, and scant evidence indicates that being fat is ever purely a "lifestyle choice." It is a mark of the othering of fat bodies that we spend as much time as we do wondering why fat people are fat while we spend much less time wondering why thinner bodies are the size they are.

Seeing fat people first and foremost as created in the Divine image allows us to cut a clear path right through the quagmire of debates about how fat people come to be fat. It demands that we recognize that human beings are infinitely worthy of respectful, competent care regardless of our size. The cause of our needs does not determine our worthiness.

When people cite Mishnah Sanhedrin as a starting point for talking about what we mean by being created *b'tzelem Elohim*, the fact that the human being in question is on trial for murder often fades into the background. But when it comes to asserting fat people's humanity, I think this is actually a point to be foregrounded: the worth of a human life is not conditioned on a person's goodness or lack thereof. Being *b'tzelem Elohim* is not an earned status or one that we can "sin away."

We do not have to play the good fatty to accrue human dignity. I once asked my family doctor about an odd set of test results I had received. "What does it mean," I wanted to know, "that this criterion is in the reference range while this other related one is high?" Without explaining anything about the tests or the biomarkers in question, she said, "It means you have good genes and bad behavior." But she had never asked me about any of my behaviors, nor had she done any tests to measure genetic factors. She was looking at my fat body and making assumptions about what my behaviors were based on my size.

Fatness is not a behavior. And you cannot know what anyone's behaviors are by looking at their size. However, what we learn from our Mishnah is that even people who are facing the consequences of their bad behavior (i.e., being tried for murder) are still deserving of human dignity. To be blunt, fat people are *b'tzelem Elohim* even if you think we are murdering ourselves with our "lifestyle choice" of fatness.

Our embodiment of the Divine image is not diminished even if our fatness is bad for our health, our own damn fault, something we could change if we wanted to, the result of "bad lifestyle choices," a moral failing, or even a "death sentence." Fat people's humanity overrides your judgments of our morality, as well as your so-called concerns for our health.

Fat People Are Partners with God in Creation

To be human, in Jewish tradition, also means to have the potential to partner with God in the ongoing work of creation. We are not meant to be merely the objects of other people's decisions and judgments, but subjects with our own, albeit limited, authority. We are world shapers, authors of reality, not only its "content."

From this flows body autonomy: the right and the responsibility to be the ones who make choices about our own bodies. Fat people are too often stripped of our sovereignty over the entire world of each of our own unique bodies. From a multibillion-dollar global weight-loss industry, to well-meaning doctors pushing treatments on us without allowing us fully informed consent, to the unsolicited advice of everyone from dear family members to complete strangers on the street, fat people are constantly subjected to other people's ideas about how we ought to "do something" about the apparent emergencies of our bodies.

In my early twenties, a few years into my own journey of fat acceptance, I paid a visit to a family friend on the West Coast. She had known me all my life but had not seen me since I had stopped dieting in my teens. She welcomed me into her living room, and I was sitting on a comfortable couch. But I became less and less comfortable as I slowly started to feel like I was being interviewed. It became clear that my hostess was asking me about my size under the guise of "being concerned about my health."

I went a few rounds with her, trying to explain that I took a non-dieting approach to health and feeling like I needed to be a cheerful ambassador from the strange country of fat acceptance. But she seemed intent on continuing the conversation. Perhaps she thought she could wear down my resistance to her completely unwanted intrusion. I was certainly feeling worn down, and I started wondering when (or now perhaps if) my luggage and I would be shown to a room with a door that closed. In a last-ditch effort to end the conversation, I dug deep, re-upped my smile, and blurted out, "I would rather die young than spend another day on a diet."

While it remains unclear how old a fat person has to get before their death can be blamed on anything other than their size, I have no desire to die young. My desire is to be allowed to make my own choices about my body. And that birthright desire overrides any arguments—scientific, pseudoscientific, and otherwise—about conflicting approaches to fat people's health.

I am often asked whether I think people should be allowed to try to lose weight or whether someone can claim to be an advocate for fat liberation and still wish their body were smaller. Depending on the nature of our relationship, I may want to explore with you the reasons behind your decision to diet or even make sure that you are aware of the risks involved. But I would no sooner try to forbid a fellow human being from dieting than I would forbid a fellow human being from cliff diving. I cannot hold that my body is mine without also believing that your body is yours. Hillel famously taught: "What is hateful to you do not do to another" (BT Shabbat 31a). It is specifically because of how hateful to me the regular intrusions on my own autonomy are that I try hard not to intrude on the autonomy of others.

Meanwhile, the intrusions on fat people's own autonomy are a constant threat. Many of these unwanted interactions are initiated by family, friends, or others who purport to actually care about us. I feel lucky that, over thirty years on in my fat acceptance journey, this is almost never true for me anymore. However, I am not at all protected from street harassment, most commonly in the form of unsolicited weight-loss advice from strangers. Sometimes, this advice is very clearly an attack, as when my husband and I were crossing a street and a woman crossed in the opposite direction, then stopped in the crosswalk to look back at us, and yelled, "Go get the surgery!" before walking on.

More often, input about my size comes from folks who genuinely think they are being friendly and helpful. One such person stopped me on the pedestrian path on which we were both walking to let me know that she believed the key to weight loss was walking and that I should really try it. She paused, clearly expecting me to respond gratefully, as if she were not a complete stranger who blocked my path while I was *walking* to tell me that I ought to try *walking*. Even while we are being accosted, we are not truly seen for who we are.

Even when our lived experience as fat people is being lived right in front of you, even when we tell you all about it, you often do not believe what we go through. I was hosting Shabbat dinner a number of years ago for a group of rabbinical students, as well as a beloved teacher of mine. This was shortly before Fat Torah's public coming-out, and I was talking to my students about how just walking out the door of my house and into the world as a fat person, knowing the kind of street harassment that often awaits me, could be an act of resistance.

Of course, I told my students, it would be wonderful if this were not so and if I had the option of walking around in my body mindlessly. And, certainly, no one should feel obligated to make meaning, activist or otherwise, out of their own oppression. However, I felt, and I still feel, that there are real ways for people with derided, marginalized bodies (fat and otherwise) to practice being ourselves in public as a form of activism, if we so choose.

I was wondering aloud at the Shabbat dinner table about what it might be like to create a space for students from abroad, who were learning in Israel for an extended period of time, to reflect on this form of resistance together, learning from and supporting one another. I told them of my sense of regret around not having shared this with past cohorts of students and how much I looked forward to creating this possibility moving forward. I felt so uplifted by my own daring in newly broaching this subject with rabbinical students and by their enthusiasm for helping me develop this idea.

So imagine how my bubble burst the next day when I was talking with my dear teacher, who had been silent through this part of our dinner. "Do strangers on the street really make comments about your size?" my teacher asked somewhat innocently. "Yes," I answered, gobsmacked and deflated, "they really do." A central figure in my own rabbinic training and a deep thinker about the interplay between God, society, and our personal lives—how could this person be so clueless about the lived experience of so many fat people?!?

It seems that all around the perpetrators of street harassment and their targets is a sea of clueless bystanders, some of whom never even see what is going on. They do not notice unless someone tells them what is happening, and even then they may not believe it. Not only are we rendered invisible, but so are the humiliations we suffer. It is not surprising that fat people, like so many other victims of violence of all sorts, are wary of telling our stories. Being disbelieved deepens the dehumanizing wound.

Seizing our human birthright as authors of our own stories also means insisting that our stories be listened to and believed. In a piece called "On the Epistemology of Fatness," Cat Pausé, a fat activist and fat studies scholar, wrote, "Fat people are the ones who know best about their lives, their behaviours, and their experiences. Fat people are knowers, and fat people know. Fat people produce knowledge."[5]

One important form of knowledge production is that fat people get to decide what is fatphobic. Too often we are expected to sit through "fat jokes," and when we do speak up we are then told not to take it personally. This is a double objectification: bodies like ours are the object of the joke; we ought to at least be believed when we name the painfulness of this reality.

Our self-authoring is also constrained when others make assumptions about us. Among the fat acceptance slogans already on the scene when I joined the movement in the 1990s was the bumper sticker (or T-shirt or button or poster, take your pick) "How dare you assume I'd rather be thin?"—presumably inspired by the classic gay liberation slogan "How dare you assume I'm straight?"

Worse still is having words put in our mouth or in some cases right in our medical records. A gastroenterologist who recommended that I lose weight seemed stumped when I asked him if he had a suggestion of a proven, safe, and sustainable method for doing so. He admitted that he did not, but it still seemed important to him to be able to write in his report that I had agreed that I would try to lose weight. When I did not agree to do so, he simply ended the appointment by saying, "Okay, well, I'll just write down that you're going to try to eat fewer carbs." I had not expressed any such intention. All these moments of being intruded upon, disbelieved, and disempowered undermine fat people's opportunities for being the authors of our own lives.

Naming Ourselves

One particular kind of partnering with God in the ongoing work of creation is the work of naming ourselves. In Torah, God begins creating the world through naming it—calling the brightness "day" and the darkness "night" (Genesis 1:5) and so on—but then God brings each living creature to the human being, and "whatever the human called every living creature, that was its name" (Genesis 2:19).

In Bamidbar, a collection of texts interpreting biblical verses, we find a *midrash* that imagines that, in addition to naming the animals, the first human also chose their own name: "[God] said to [Adam], 'And you, what is your name?' Adam said, 'Adam, because I was created out of the earth (*adamah*)'" (Bamidbar Rabbah 19:3).

Fat people's humanity too includes this power to name ourselves. One of the boldest acts is naming ourselves "fat," taking a word that is used as an accusation or a slur and deciding that this word is actually ours to use and to make meaning of. As so many other marginalized people—including Jews—have found, reclaiming a word that has been used as a slur is a way for fat people to wrest the power of this word away from those who use it to harm us. Since at least 1967, fat activists have been engaged in the project of using the word "fat" as a morally neutral descriptor of fat people's bodies. In addition to being ripe for reclamation, "fat" is accurate, non-euphemistic, and free from medicalizing stigma. Calling ourselves "fat" can even be world changing.

"Fat" accurately describes a particular body size and type in the great diversity of human forms. And the accuracy of the word "fat" is only problematic when fatness is stigmatized, even in subtle ways. When my daughter was in kindergarten, one of her teachers invited me to come in so that I could see some of what she was learning. The teacher asked us to play a game together in which I had to close my eyes while my kid flipped over one of the two cards on the table in front of me. When I opened my eyes, I had to say which card she had flipped and what was different about the image on this side of the card. In front of me was one card with a picture of a chicken and another card with a picture of a tree. I closed my eyes and, when I opened them, the chicken card had been flipped over to reveal a fatter chicken. I said, "You flipped the chicken card and I can tell because this chicken is fatter and the other one was thinner." My daughter nodded her approval confidently, but her teacher blushed and quickly corrected me, saying, "Yes, this chicken is . . . *bigger.*"

But "bigger" didn't really make sense. The chicken wasn't taller. It wasn't some overall larger type of chicken. It wasn't an enlarged image of the same skinny chicken. It was just a fattened version of

Every Body Beloved | 75

the same fowl. "Fatter" was the most accurate description of the difference between the two birds, yet the teacher reacted as if I had said something offensive. Perhaps she was concerned for the chicken's feelings? In a world without anti-fat bias, we would all feel free to use the word "fat" as a spot-on descriptor of some types of bodies in the divine variety of human (and chicken) forms.

Because we are not yet in that fat-liberated reality, reclaiming the term "fat" by using it in a neutral or positive way—taking as our own a term that has been used to marginalize us—can be immediately world changing. I encouraged others to take on this challenge in a grant proposal I wrote, in which I was asked to describe how I thought Fat Torah effected change. After I had summarized our programs and talked about how we measure impact, I wrote:

> In a world where fatness is denigrated and fat people are consistently devalued as human beings, simply saying aloud the words "Fat Torah" is a bold action that effects immediate change (Try it!).

We did not get the grant. But I stand by my position that choosing to use the word "fat" in a positive, or even a neutral, way still remains a radical act. Echoing similar reclamations of the words "queer" or "Jew" or "autistic," reclaiming an identity marker that is still so often used to shame us is a way of making it clear to ourselves and others that we have nothing to be ashamed of.

"Fat" can also be quite shocking, both for those of us who are still getting used to saying it and for those hearing it. This shock value should not be underestimated. Using the word "fat" in a morally neutral way upsets the status quo. If you have not tried it yet, be prepared for it to be exciting and scary. "Fat" names what is otherwise unspeakable; it centralizes what is marginalized; it gives voice to what others would silence. Shocking, indeed!

Personally, I also prefer using the word "fat" over using euphemisms, especially those that aim to be cute or humorous. Euphemisms are often used to "correct" fat people when we use the word "fat" to describe ourselves, as in "You're not fat, you're fluffy." The hope here seems to be that cuteness or humor can deflect stigma. But no amount of "fluffy" or "curvy" can truly conceal the underlying bias against fatness in these words. That said, each of us is entitled to refer to ourselves with the words of our own choosing. If you prefer to call yourself "fluffy," I am not here to take it away from you.

I am sometimes asked what I think of the term "zaftig." While in Yiddish this word literally means "juicy," in English, or Yinglish, usage, it has come to refer to a woman's body that is "pleasantly plump." If you love having a Yinglish word for your body and you feel you fit the description, please keep being your wonderful zaftig self. For me, I feel that zaftig is a highly gendered and (hetero)sexualized term that has never really referred to people who are my size of fat. Additionally, "zaftig" to me seems wrapped up in stereotypes of Jewish bodies generally and Jewish women's bodies in particular. And, even though the term is meant to be one of endearment, I remain wary of supporting the idea that there is such a thing as a type of body that is "Jewish."

None of this is to say that I enjoy being called "fat" by people who are still using the word as a slur. Shifting the word's meaning—defanging it—can take practice even for those of us with the best intent. A clergy person in one Fat Torah workshop very vulnerably shared that, because of the way the word "fat" had been used against them, they still were not comfortable using it neutrally, even though, intellectually, they fully supported doing so. If you are in this same spot and cannot yet use "fat" neutrally, some other options might be "larger bodied," "higher weight," or "plus size."

"Fat" is a word for "us" to use in describing ourselves; it is not anyone else's to use to reinforce a world in which we are only "them." To borrow a slogan from the world of disability justice, "Nothing about us without us." Using the word "fat" to describe our own bodies lays claim to our right, as human beings created in the image of God, to determine what fat and fatness mean.

All of this naming of ourselves happens against the backdrop of how we are commonly referred to by others. I am thinking here especially not of outright slurs but of the everyday terms in which fat bodies are described, what many of us refer to as the *O* words—namely, "overweight" and "obese." Each of these is problematic for their own reasons. We might even say that the *O* stands for "othering."

"Overweight" is perhaps the most common term for fat people, and it implies that there is some other weight, some other person, that we are supposed to be. When you call me overweight, you let me know that you see me as existing out of the bounds of who I ought to be. "Overweight" also forgets the "unique" part about being created in the Divine image, giving preference to the idea that there is a standard weight against which all people should be measured.

"Obese" assumes disease; it medicalizes a body size. There is a big difference between being a human being with a whole profile of potentially increased risks for certain disease processes and decreased risks for others and the dehumanization of being seen as the embodiment of disease itself. The etymology of "obese" is equally troubling. It comes from a Latin word that means "to have eaten oneself to fatness." Once again we find here assumptions about fat people's behavior without any curiosity about what our actual behaviors might be.

Some, especially those trying to decrease weight stigma in order to get more fat people to buy their weight-loss products, have suggested shifting to person-first language for fat people, referring to us as "person with overweight" or "person with obesity." This kind of language further strengthens the notion that fatness is in and of itself a disease. It tries to distance our personhood from our fatness, when it is only bias that makes this seem necessary. I do not want to be seen as a human being "despite" my fatness. I am a whole person, fatness and all.

Ultimately, the act of choosing what to call myself, using the much-maligned "fat" as a neutral descriptor of my body size, is itself an assertion that I am created in the image of the Divine. Naming ourselves lets us embody our own humanity by being subjects with voices, not merely objects for others to assess and judge. When I call myself fat, I am self-authoring, telling my own story. In a world that constantly objectifies fat bodies—treating us as a joke to be laughed at or as a woe to be lamented—picking our own descriptors and defining the meaning of those descriptors is an act of taking back that power. Calling myself "fat," without apologizing for my size, sometimes even with a big fat smile on my face, builds a tiny one-syllable sanctuary, a miniature momentary world, in which fatness is no longer denigrated or despised.

Naming God

The *midrash* in which the first human being chooses their own name goes on to see in the human being the power to name God as well: "The blessed Holy One said to him, 'I, what is My name?' Adam said, 'The Lord (Adonai), because you are Lord over all creatures,' namely as written (Isaiah 42:8), 'I am the Lord, that is My name.'"

Naming God can also be a fat liberatory process; engaging with our own theology is also fat people's birthright as humans. We too can play with ascribing to God positive qualities that we associate with fatness. We can elevate the divine qualities of abundance, vastness, softness, amorphousness, *Ḥesed* (lovingkindness) as unboundedness, and *Gedulah* (greatness) as largeness. We can ask, "What might be divine about fatness?" and "How is God fat?"

Theology is a deeply personal practice, and I am especially shy of being prescriptive here or of falling merely into stereotypes of fatness. But there is so much room for engaging in the human practice of naming who we want and need God to be. As we are reflections of God's image, our own image of who God is can reflect our bodies and our knowing.

The Rabbi at the Bathhouse

Another expression of what it means to be created *b'tzelem Elohim* appears in Vayikra Rabbah (34:3). There, a story is told about how the students of Hillel liked to walk with him when he was taking leave of them:

> They said to him, "Rabbi, where are you walking to?" He said to them, "To fulfill a commandment!" They said to him, "And what commandment is this?" He said to them, "To bathe in the

> bathhouse." They said to him: "But is this really a commandment?" He said to them: "Yes. Just like regarding the statues of kings, that are set up in the theaters and the circuses, the one who is appointed over them bathes them and scrubs them, and they give him sustenance, and furthermore, he attains status with the leaders of the kingdom; I, who was created in the [Divine] Image and Form, as it is written, 'For in the Image of God He made Man (Genesis 9:6),' even more so!"

We can imagine that it must have been shocking to Hillel's students to learn that he was bathing his body in a Roman bathhouse. But he was teaching that just as the caregivers of statues of human kings treat those forms with respect, we caregivers of our own human bodies need to recognize how these bodies, created *b'tzelem Elohim*, are worthy of honor and exquisite care just the way they are.

Too often we can barely even identify with our own fatness. We are told to wish it away as if it were ephemeral, a stumbling block to the "more real" identity of thinness that is waiting for us right around the corner of the next new and improved "lifestyle choice." As we already said, person-first language and the emphasis on obesity as a disease reinforce this, as if my fatness is something added on to an otherwise nonfat self.

Too often we are treated as if we should have shown up in some other body. This is particularly deeply felt when medical professionals have trouble assessing our bodies the way they expect to. At its worst, this tendency can be genuinely harmful in terms of accessing competent medical care.

You know those cute pictures of fetuses in utero that pregnant people share? When ultrasound techs would show me the pictures they had printed out of my babies in the womb, they would expertly point out the features—here's the head and here's one leg and another leg—and I would look at the printout and say, with full honesty, "That looks like a plate of mashed potatoes."

But at least those techs were being kind about the fact that, for some fat folks, ultrasounds, during pregnancy and otherwise, do not produce images that are as clear as those of thinner bodies. Inevitably, this lack of clarity is blamed on the fat person instead of on the technology or on the person operating the technology.

One particularly bad ultrasound encounter was the first "anatomy scan" during my first pregnancy. The well-regarded Dr. T was not having a good day even before I walked into his office. He seemed to have a cold, his computer wasn't working right, and he did not seem to have much confidence in, or basic rapport with, his assistant. And he had a very hard time seeing all the parts that he wanted to view of the fetus I was growing. He was rude to me, making it clear that his job would have been much easier if I had had the decency to show up in a different, thinner body. And he wrote in his report that the test was limited due to the shape of my body. But this is incorrect. The results were limited due to the limits of the technology to properly visualize a body like mine. Your machine, your technique, or the combination of the two led to the limits of your ability to see what you wanted to see.

If Not Now, When?

Fat people should be treated as full human beings with the bodies we have today. I do not have some other body I can run home and get. This body right now is created in the Divine image. Hillel was not claiming that there was something special or particularly wonderful about his body. He was just acknowledging that to be *b'tzelem Elohim* means to be worthy of attentive, respectful care.

Every Body Beloved | 85

We are not born in the Divine image and then ruined somehow. The Divine image does not have problem areas. Your whole body, the entire terrain of you, is in the Divine image. People have all kinds of stories they tell about how they got to be fat. But, when it comes to human dignity, it really does not matter. Your body size is not an error.

"In your goodness," we say of God in our daily prayers, "You renew the works of creation every day." Fat bodies too are created anew each day. Whatever body you woke up in this morning was created in the Divine image.

In a world of standardized sizes of so many things (clothes, seating, MRI machines, etc.) it can be easy to feel like the size of our body is wrong. But the size of the body is never wrong. It may be a mismatch. But a mismatch is not the same as a mistake or a wrongness or an evil.

The ways that we "don't fit" are societal failures to properly recognize, honor, and care for the image of God. Can't find clothes that fit? That is society and the clothing industry choosing not to properly adorn every size of the Divine image. Been told in a job interview—in that horribly fatphobic (and often racist and classist) coded term—that you were "unpolished?" That right there is a lack of appreciation of the many forms of "polished" and "unpolished" that God's image comes in. Sent for a much-needed MRI only to find that the machine is too small? Try saying to yourself, "This is a failure to provide proper care for the Divine image." There is no "wrong way" to embody the image of God, with its minute-by-minute, lifelong umbilical connection to the womb of creation.

To the kid who drew a picture of me to hurt my daughter's feelings

The first I heard about what you had done was a message from your mother saying that you had behaved toward B in a hurtful way. When I asked B if she could tell me what happened, she shyly told me that you had drawn a picture of me with no hair and no clothes and had shown it to her to make fun of her. "And that wasn't nice," she concluded firmly. I calmly told her that I agreed that it wasn't nice at all and that I would be in touch with your parents to figure out what we were going to do about it.

I was proud that I was able to stay calm with her; my interactions with B around this incident are about her experience of the situation, not mine. But underneath that calm I could feel swirling currents of sadness and anger and hurt. It hurts when my body is made fun of. It hurts a hundred times worse to know that my body is being made fun of in order to hurt my child. Also, it was creepy:

Where in your sweet little head could there possibly live an image of me with no hair and no clothes?!?

When I spoke to your mother, I learned some things that changed my understanding of what happened and what it might mean. She told me that you yourself have been made fun of by kids who derisively call you "fat." You know how painful that is, and on reflection, you were deeply upset that you had hurt B's feelings. I am proud of you for being able to use your own experience to imagine how you must have made B feel. Even though you knew it would be hard, you had already committed—with your parents' guidance and support—to making a full apology to B the next day in school and to asking her if there was anything else you could do to make things right.

You and B have known each other since preschool; as three-year-olds you would often walk around holding hands. Once, somewhere around that age, B bit you hard, and while you seemed to make a full and quick recovery from the incident, she was so upset by her own behavior that she was still crying when I picked her up at the end of the day. You two are on this amazing journey—along with your peers and with all the rest of us too—of figuring out what it means to be human and how to relate to other human beings. We are all in this together, this ongoing experiment in how we hurt ourselves and one another and how we can possibly heal.

Your mother also told me that you love to draw pictures of sumo wrestlers, and the picture you drew was actually one of your beloved gigantic warriors, to which you had then added the words "B's mom" underneath. I was immediately relieved when I heard this; it lessened the creepiness considerably to know that the mostly hairless, nearly naked person you had drawn did not start out having anything to do with my own body.

When I was teased for being fat, starting in second grade, just like you are, I believed the premise of the teasing; I believed that being fat was a bad thing. I was put down, and I bought into the idea that my body was worthy of putting down. Even though it still always hurts to be made fun of for being fat, it does make a difference that today I no longer believe there is anything wrong with my fatness. This deep knowing is a bulwark against the breakers of emotional pain and upheaval. So when I learned what you had actually drawn, my heart still ached, but my humongous inner warrior spirit shone a little brighter. "Fuck yeah, I'm a sumo wrestler!" I thought to myself, happy to associate my body with such a bold image of fat strength.

My deepest wish for you is that you can come to share my faith in the possibility of healing our relationships with fatness and bodies—our own and everyone else's. The drawing that you made and the caption that you gave it put me in mind of the teaching from Rebbe Nachman: "If you believe it is possible to do damage, [you must] believe it is possible to repair" (Likutei Moharan, Part II: 112:1).

You took an image of a sumo wrestler—a fat figure you admire—and used a caption underneath it to belittle B for having a fat mom. The way you titled the picture impacted most people's ability to see it for the proud warrior's body it initially was.

I hope no one else ever makes fun of your body again. But if they do, I hope you are able to do the opposite of what you did with that picture of "me." Even though you may still feel the sting of the attack, I want you to know that you can reject the painful meaning that is being handed to you.

Choose a different caption.

Write a different story about how it is to have whatever body you have.

Tell us all what it means to *you* to be you.

3

Taking Good Care

When I started more publicly asserting that fat people too are created in the image of God, I knew that one milestone in measuring the reach of this message would be the arrival of "concern trolling"—attacks in the guise of caring about well-being. This helpful quote is often misattributed to Gandhi: "First they ignore you, then they laugh at you, then they fight you, then you win." However, for those of us advocating for the humanity of fat people, a step is missing in this progression. It should say, "First they ignore you, then they laugh at you, then they pretend to care about your health. . . ."

When the trolls arrived, they were in fine form. In response to a lovely article[1] about Fat Torah and other efforts at faith-based fat activism, one commenter wrote, "There is never a reason to celebrate being overweight," while another made it even clearer that hers was a "nonjudgmental" concern: "Not to judge people on the basis of size or weight . . . but let's not celebrate unhealthy behavior."

When it comes to fat people, suddenly everyone is a crusading public health advocate using the language of "caring" to do anything but that. Caring is in the eyes, and the heart, of the cared for. In the more than four decades that loved ones, healthcare providers, and complete strangers have expressed concern about my fatness using some variation on the question "But what about your health?" I have not once experienced this concern as caring. To be told I am being cared for when I feel that the opposite is true is gaslighting, pure and simple. My emotions and my nervous system have only ever experienced it as just another bullying attack.

True Caring

The first hint that offers of concern for fat people's health are not actually caring—whether they come from people who actually know us or from random strangers on the internet—is that they are usually offered without our consent. A series of stories in Talmud (BT Berakhot 5b) is often used to discuss the topics of suffering, caring, and receiving care. In these stories, one rabbi falls ill and another rabbi comes to offer healing. We read first of Rabbi Yoḥanan, a famed healer, visiting his sick student. I feel compelled to mention that Rabbi Yoḥanan was also famous for being very fat and very beautiful, but that's another story. In our story, Rabbi Yoḥanan begins by asking his ailing pupil, "Are your sufferings welcome to you?" When his student, Rabbi Ḥiyya bar Abba, answers that he welcomes neither his sufferings nor any supposed reward he might get for them, Rabbi Yoḥanan says, "Give me your hand." The healer takes his student's hand and "raises him up," healing him.

In the next story, Rabbi Yoḥanan himself becomes ill, and another student of his, Rabbi Ḥanina, comes to visit. The same dialogue repeats itself, this time with Rabbi Ḥanina asking his teacher if his sufferings are welcome to him and Rabbi Yoḥanan saying they are not. Rabbi Ḥanina instructs his teacher to give him his hand, and Rabbi Yoḥanan is healed. The Talmud wonders why Rabbi Yoḥanan could not heal himself, given his known prowess as a healer. "A prisoner," the text concludes, "cannot free himself from prison."

When this text is taught, the emphasis is often put on its moving message of interdependence. Even the most powerful healer needs to be cared for in order to heal. But what strikes me when I think of how much concern is expressed about fat people's health is the very first question that the healing visitor asks in each story: "Are your sufferings welcome to you?" In other words, "May I offer you help?" Every one of us needs helping hands at many different points in our lives, but true concern—and helping and healing—starts with consent.

Additionally, true caring means meeting people where they are and addressing *their* concerns, not only your own. Even if you are an actual health expert, you cannot accurately assess a person's health just by looking at their fat body. When people tell me they are concerned about my health without knowing what my own health concerns, or lack thereof, might be, they are not truly seeing me.

In one Ḥassidic tale, a rabbi learns something about true caring when he sees two men drinking together. The first asks his drinking buddy, "Do you love me?" "Of course, I love you so so much!" replies his inebriated companion. "No," the first one insists, "you cannot possibly love me because you don't know what hurts me." When you are concerned about my health without knowing anything about my health, about what does or does not "hurt me," I do not experience it as caring.

Addressing my concerns and not only one's own should hold true even for healthcare providers. Sadly, it does not. At my six-week postpartum checkup after my second pregnancy, my gynecologist told me that I needed to lose weight. He did not mention any specific concerns about how he saw my size impacting my health, nor did he inquire about any concerns I might have. He just seemed to feel, as most doctors do, that it was good practice to tell a fat person that they are fat and that they should really try not to be. We went a few rounds, with me explaining why I was not interested in pursuing intentional weight loss. Somehow, eventually, we moved on.

Had that been the end of the visit, I would likely have just chalked it up to one more healthcare provider who feels the need to tell me to lose weight without explaining in a satisfactory way either why I should pursue intentional weight loss or how to do so in a way that is proven to be safe and effective in the long term. But then, later in the same visit, I asked my doctor whether he could write me a referral for a test of my thyroid function. In my previous pregnancy, I had lost thyroid function, so during this pregnancy—since being pregnant can both impact the thyroid and, in turn, be impacted by it—the maternal-fetal health specialist I had been seeing up until I gave birth made sure my thyroid function was closely monitored. Now that I was breastfeeding again, I wanted to be sure we continued to keep a close eye on this actual health indicator especially because low thyroid function can cause low milk supply.

My gynecologist flatly refused my request, saying, "You can get that referral from your family doctor. The thyroid is not a gynecological organ." I cannot know his actual intentions, but the impression this doctor left me with was that he was concerned about my fat body when it came to recommending weight loss for unspecified reasons, but my specific needs around the healthy functioning of my (fat) lactating breasts were somehow outside of his area of concern. This physician felt called to swerve out of his lane in order to recommend weight loss without me asking for his help in that area. Declining to help me with what I *was* concerned about highlights the unevenness, the rocky ground, of the supposedly caring attention that fat people face.

Even if you have my consent to talk about my health, and even if you know what my own concerns are, true caring means respecting my bodily autonomy—the freedom and responsibility to make my own choices about my body. The bottom line is that caring is best assessed by the supposedly cared for. The negative impact on my overall well-being from those purporting to care matters more than any potentially good intentions they might have. You cannot claim to care about my health if I experience your every expression of caring as its opposite.

Is "Being Healthy" a *Mitzvah*?

When the trolling started, I began to notice that some comments came from people who expressed specifically Jewish concerns about fat people's health. Often these commenters would swap out "But what about your health?" for "But what about *shmirat hanefesh*?" If this is the first time you have heard of the *mitzvah* of *shmirat hanefesh*, please know that I had never heard of this Jewish religious obligation either. Sometimes being a rabbi feels like one long moment of being made aware of all the things you did not learn in rabbinical school.

I have found that when someone points at what I fear is a lacuna in my rabbinic education, my best bet is to put my learning hat on and head to the books. We make Torah our own not by rigidly clinging to what we already know but by embracing the ongoing process of studying and wrestling with the tradition. I am blessed to learn with the same *chevruta* (study partner) I've had since our second year of rabbinical school. He was game, so we took our question of "What is *shmirat hanefesh*?" and jumped into the "sea of Talmud"—the vast tradition of learning Jewish texts.

We quickly learned that *shmirat hanefesh*, which means "taking care of yourself," is a *mitzvah* that uses a verse from Deuteronomy as its prooftext. "*V'nishmartem me'od l'nafshoteikhem*," the verse begins, urging us to "Take very good care of yourselves" (Deuteronomy 4:15). It is worth noting that the meaning of the word *nefesh* changes over time. In biblical Hebrew, *nefesh* means a living being—human or animal; biblical Hebrew makes no distinction between body and soul, nor does it explicitly imbue human beings with a "self." Under the influence of Greek philosophy, rabbinic Judaism does begin developing an idea of body and soul as potentially separate "parts" of one human being, but this never coalesces into a doctrinal or fixed definition of what the soul is or how the body/soul/self relationship needs to be construed. In this context, *nefesh* comes to be used as one of a number of words for the soul/spirit/lifeforce—each with its own nuanced set of meanings—in the Jewish mystical and spiritual traditions.

This potential interpretive openness in various times and places, along with the ongoing presence of the biblical text itself, can allow for varied meanings of the opening words of our verse in Deuteronomy. More broadly, how each of us sees the relationships between our bodies and any other aspects of ourselves can impact what we think it means to "take care of yourself."

It also feels important to point out here that there is a difference between a *mitzvah*—a commandment to "do this" or "don't do that" in Jewish law (*halakhah*)—and a broader universalist moral obligation. None of us are, from a more universal moral standpoint, obligated either to be healthy—which is impossible since "being healthy" is not actually a behavior or set of behaviors—or even to try to pursue being healthy. Health is not an achievement, moral or otherwise, and illness is not a failure. Similarly, "being healthy" cannot possibly be a *mitzvah* since *mitzvot* are all actions that we are called upon either to "get up and do" or to "sit down and refrain from doing."

One way of thinking of *mitzvot* is that these obligations are the marriage contract—mutually agreed upon terms in a loving relationship—between God and the Jews. Aspiring to adhere to *halakhah* is not everyone's idea of what being Jewish is all about. Still, for many Jews, taking on the "yoke" of the *mitzvot*, out of our own human free will, remains central to Jewish adulthood. *Mitzvot* matter to me, though I see them as something I take upon myself as a devotional practice rather than viewing them as a legal code that I will somehow be punished for violating. So if someone tells me that pursuing health is a "positive commandment" (i.e., one of the "get up and do it" *mitzvot*), I take that seriously. The question of "what about *shmirat hanefesh*?" made me curious to know more about this *mitzvah*.

Was my call for fat people to be recognized as human beings somehow in conflict with *shmirat hanefesh*, as some online commenters and direct message correspondents claimed? And how would this impact my thinking, my rabbinate, and my life's work if it was?

Healthism, but in Hebrew

In contemporary usage, if my concern trolls and Google were to be believed, *shmirat hanefesh* is mostly used to put a Jewish patina on plain old anti-fat bias and healthism. Coined by economist Robert

Crawford in his 1980 article "Healthism and the Medicalization of Everyday Life,"[2] healthism is "the preoccupation with personal health as a primary—often the primary—focus for the definition and achievement of well-being; a goal which is to be attained primarily through the modification of life styles." Crawford's concern is that healthism ignores social determinants of health and necessarily limits the pursuit of health to people with the wealth to do so. In addition to anti-fat bias, we can also think about how racism, ableism, misogyny, ageism, and other oppressive structures make healthism worse.

In popular usage, *shmirat hanefesh* is used to sell all kinds of contemporary ideas about wellness and fitness, again with an emphasis on these as achievements as opposed to outcomes of a complex set of causes including genetics, social determinants of health, and an individual's placement on various measures of privilege and oppression. This is not to say that *shmirat hanefesh* is always used nefariously. It has been used to promote vaccination among the *ḥaredi* (ultraorthodox) population as well as to encourage mask wearing during the COVID-19 pandemic. There have been halakhic discussions among Orthodox scholars about whether smoking is prohibited by Jewish law because it violates *shmirat hanefesh*. And any number of well-meaning efforts to provide a Jewish framework for the pursuit of mental and physical health draw on the biblical principle of "Take good care of yourselves."

However, this principle is also used to sell diets, to encourage "juice cleanses," and to promote dubious exercise schemes. It is too easily wedded to racist, classist, anti-fat, and anti-femme diet culture and wellness culture. Indeed, whenever the pursuit of health slides over into non-evidence-based territory—not to mention outright quackery—*shmirat hanefesh* is right there to wrap up ableism and healthism in halakhic bows.

Medieval Science and *Shmirat Haguf*

In addition to applying *shmirat hanefesh* to contemporary ideas about health-promoting behaviors, some also like to take actual health advice from older Jewish sources. Maimonides, the twelfth-century rabbi, physician, and philosopher, is a favorite in this regard. He makes it clear that maintaining our physical health is a must because, in his words, "one cannot understand or have any knowledge of the Creator, if he is ill, therefore, he must avoid that which harms the body and accustom himself to that which is healthful and helps the body become stronger" (Mishneh Torah, Human Dispositions 4:1).

Those who cite this in talking about *shmirat hanefesh*—or use our Deuteronomy verse but refer to the *mitzvah* in question as *shmirat haguf* (taking care of the body, specifically)—often also use the immediate continuation of the Mishneh Torah text as actual health advice: "A person should never eat unless he is hungry, nor drink unless thirsty. He should never put off relieving himself, even for an instant. Rather, whenever he needs to urinate or move his bowels, he should do so immediately."

This seems fair enough, but two concerning things are happening here from my perspective. First, there is a cherry-picking of Maimonides's health advice as if to praise Jewish wisdom for knowing about how to take good care of our bodies even eight hundred years ago. The problem with this is that it fails to quote the continuation of the text in Mishneh Torah where Maimonides goes on to talk about other ways to avoid harming the body: never eat mushrooms; avoid fruits (except figs, grapes, and almonds); bloodletting is acceptable but never in summer or winter, only a little bit in the spring and the fall.

Maimonides further promises that anyone who follows his health plan "will not become ill throughout his life, until he reaches advanced age and dies. He will not need a doctor. His body will remain intact and healthy throughout his life."

I am not faulting Maimonides for using his best understanding of the science of the day to try to help people take care of themselves. However, I do find fault with the practice of promoting both his health advice and his understanding of physical health as an achievement and as a prerequisite for serving God. Science changes, and maybe one day the current science will align with some more of Maimonides's points. Maybe it really is bad for you to have sex when you are too hungry or too full, as he insists. But what has started changing—though plenty more change is still needed—is our ability to listen to the voices of the disabled and the "unhealthy" and understand that a particular ideal of health is not required to serve our Creator.

Taking Risks

If we want to keep *shmirat hanefesh*, and not just cede it to those who use it as an oppressive cudgel, we need to dig deeper still. One classic framing of *shmirat hanefesh* in Jewish tradition is that of practicing self-preservation or avoiding unnecessary risks. Rather than a blanket obligation to avoid risk, however, the tradition is clear from the beginning that avoiding risks is often about choosing between different potentially risky paths.

For example, the Talmud (BT Berakhot 32b–33a) discusses various cases concerning what to do if someone tries to say hello to you when you are in the middle of praying. Under what circumstances does it make sense to interrupt our conversation with God in order to have a conversation with a person? While ideally we would be able to pray uninterrupted, failing to answer someone's greeting is potentially a threat to our safety if that person is someone with a lot of power who will expect their greeting to be acknowledged.

In one case, a Jew is praying on the road when a *hegemon*, a Roman officer, greets him. When the *ḥasid* (pious person) does not interrupt his prayer to return the officer's greeting, the *hegemon* decides to teach him a lesson. He waits until the Jew is done praying and then says, "You good-for-nothing! Doesn't your Torah say . . . 'Take very good care of yourselves?!?' and here you are ignoring my greeting?!? If I cut your head off, no one would say I was accountable [since you were so foolish as to fail to answer me]."

The *ḥasid* responds by asking the *hegemon* to think with him about the relative risks involved in this situation. "If you were standing before a human king and your buddy came along and said hello, what would happen if you turned away to answer him?" asks the *ḥasid*. The *hegemon* replies that the king would have his head cut off with a sword. "Aha!" responds the *ḥasid*, who goes on to explain that just as the risk of upsetting the human king takes precedence over the risk of upsetting your buddy, all the more so, the risk of breaking his connection with God, the Sovereign of Sovereigns, is a much greater risk in terms of *shmirat hanefesh* than the risk of upsetting a *hegemon*.

There are a few things I love about this story. First, it teaches that honoring the *mitzvah* of *shmirat hanefesh* often involves our own assessments of the risks we are willing to take. So often when we make actual choices about our well-being, we are choosing between two or more paths and doing our best to estimate the dangers and benefits of each. Second, this story highlights the fact that our well-being includes both our physical and our mental and spiritual health and that we are allowed to include risks to any of these in our choices.

Finally, when I read this story as someone who used to pursue weight loss but no longer does, I am moved by the fact that the person urging us to pay attention to our physical health (i.e., to avoid getting our head cut off with a sword) is a Roman *hegemon*. In our day, the wellness and diet industries are the *hegemony*, deeply invested—to the tune of billions of dollars—in trying to scare us into believing that our very lives are in danger if we don't automatically turn aside from whatever pursuit we are involved in to immediately pay attention to whatever soul-sucking fad they are trying to sell us. Each of us can feel empowered by this story to declare that I am too busy bowing to a deeper power that urges me to truly care for myself. For the sake of saving my sanity and perhaps my very soul, I choose to do my utmost to ignore you.

Later halakhic literature looks at the *mitzvah* of *shmirat hanefesh* as similarly involved in weighing different kinds of risk against one another. For example, one eighteenth-century *teshuvah* (a responsum, or a rabbinic answer to a question of Jewish law) from the *Noda*

108 | *Minna Bromberg*

Biyhudah takes up the question of whether Jews are allowed to hunt. While the meat of an animal that dies by being hunted is not kosher, the concern here is about the risky activity of hunting itself. The woods are full of wild beasts and other dangers. The *Noda Biyhudah*'s answer is that hunting for sport is forbidden but that hunting is permitted for those whose livelihood depends on it. If the payoff is the enjoyment of hunting, it does not outweigh the risk of the dangers to *shmirat hanefesh*. But refraining from hunting if that is your only way of making a living is not *shmirat hanefesh*.

The Risks of Dieting Versus the Risks of Not Dieting

The pursuit of weight loss is itself risky since 95 percent of attempts to lose weight result in not keeping the weight off.[3] But if these statistics are correct, this means that intentional weight loss does work 5 percent of the time. I am painting with a broom here, and it is worth noting that the chances of someone of my size becoming thin and remaining so long-term are much, much smaller.[4] But in any case, 5 percent means that if you know twenty people who have tried to lose weight, you know one person who has lost weight and kept it off. And we are conditioned to be so deeply desiring of weight loss that it is easy to focus on that five-percenter, as well as to imagine that surely we could be in that not infinitesimally small number. When anti-fat bias is such a bludgeon for fat people, it is perfectly understandable, and perhaps even "healthy," to imagine ourselves as one in that small number.

I know I have taken health risks with even smaller chances of success. When my husband and I first began seeking help with fertility, our doctor tried to warn me off by telling me just how small, in his estimation, my fat body's chances were of being able to have a baby. He took out a piece of paper and drew a graph that was meant to show odds of getting pregnant on one axis and body size on the other. And then he drew a line that presumably looked something like a line that he had seen in actual research results. The odds of getting pregnant went down and down and down as body size went up. And because of how deeply I desired motherhood, I squinted at his hand-drawn line at the far end of his size chart and thought, "Still looks like more than zero to me!"

When it comes to risk around weight loss, we tend to hear the much louder voices decrying the risks of being fat rather than actually being able to consider the risks of dieting. Attempting weight loss is bad for my mental and spiritual health, it is statistically unlikely to result in actual weight loss long-term, and the resulting weight cycling is also known to carry health risks.[5]

As the poet Robert Frost noted, we are all constrained by our ability to only "be one traveler" when two roads diverge before us. And we human beings are notoriously bad at assessing risks; we are bad at figuring out how to translate statistics into wise choices about our lives. Mostly, no matter what lottery we are playing, some part of us wants to believe that maybe this time we will be lucky. While some choices in the pursuit of weight loss are irreversible (like most surgeries), others we get to make every day. Today, I am taking very good care of myself by choosing to risk being fat rather than to risk trying not to be fat.

Idolatry

Frustrated by the various takes we were finding on just what *shmirat hanefesh* was all about, my *chevruta* and I decided to have another look at the verse in Deuteronomy. In rabbinic Judaism, halakhic (Jewish legal) decisions are meant to be made by giving the most recent arguments the most weight rather than by peeling back all the layers and looking just at their prooftexts, the biblical texts underneath. But radical ideas, like fat liberation, sometimes require radical methods. And when we look at the whole of Deuteronomy 4:15 and its continuation in the following verse, the Torah does not disappoint.

V'nishmartem me'od l'nafshoteikhem. "Take very good care of yourselves," our verse urges, and why? "Since you saw no shape when YHVH spoke to you at Horeb out of the fire, lest you act wickedly and make for yourselves a sculptured image in any likeness whatever: the form of a man or a woman."

What a retort from the text itself! This is a verse about idolatry, specifically about not idolizing a particular shape (or size) of the human body. Taking care of ourselves means making sure we are not forgetting that we ourselves stood at Sinai and heard God urging us to have no other gods but the One.

Ramban, the thirteenth-century scholar and mystic, comments on this verse that it is warning against worshiping only one aspect of God as if God's Oneness were separable. In a modern take on this, my teacher Art Green defines idolatry as "taking the part for the whole."[6]

My contention is that we can use our verse as prooftext to help us understand that healthism, anti-fat bias, and diet culture are the very idolatry that we are being warned against; they hold up a particular ideal of body size and health itself as worthy of worship and cause us to forget our inherent human wholeness. Created in the image of the Divine, each of us is a mirror, in this world, of Divine wholeness.

This warning against idolatry can be powerful no matter what we believe, or don't believe, about God—even for atheists. We have a human tendency to be worshipful, to give power over our lives to nonrational things. If we cannot stop ourselves from bowing down to one thing or another, we ought to at least be intentional about what our objects of worship are. *Shmirat hanefesh* warns us to make sure we are not worshiping physical health or a narrow definition of what constitutes an acceptable body size as an idol.

I am not being dismissive of the body and its needs and ailments. This is not a "you are not your body" argument. We are allowed to want to live long lives free of physical suffering, and we are allowed to take steps in pursuit of that. We run into trouble when we think our health is entirely up to us and when we mistake a narrow definition of physical health for the whole shebang.

One way that our tradition hints at its preference for something beyond physical health is in the liturgical practice of praying for a *refuah shleima*, a full healing, even when someone is at death's door. We do this not because we expect miracles or at least not *only* because a miracle would be nice once in a while. We pray for complete healing even when physical cure is out of the question because the true healing we seek, the true caring we can offer ourselves and one another, is the reminder of every body's inherent wholeness.

To the people at Yom Kippur services who would not move to let me through

Yom Kippur—the Day of Atonement, a day of awe and trembling and pondering our fate—is the highest attendance day at synagogues around the world. It makes sense for communities to want to fit in as many chairs as possible, expanding their seating to accommodate the larger crowd. This day and this synagogue were no different: the rows of chairs were already closer together than usual before you decided to insert an additional row in back for yourself and your friends.

My kids had clearly had enough of the worship services, and it was time to go. I found myself stuck on one side of the prayer space, trying to get my fat body through, pushing my sleepy toddler in a stroller, while my older child slipped in and out of spaces where I could not follow her. In an all too rare moment of actually advocating for myself on the spot, I took the risk of asking you to please move so that I could get to the exit ramp that your seats were blocking.

Instead of moving, you pointed to a staircase behind me and said, "Why don't you just go down there instead." For a moment I stood frozen. And then, still stunned, I tried to do what you had suggested.

My anger now rising, I bounced the stroller down the stairs to find that this exit had been blocked off using an office chair and a sideways ladder to prevent people from coming in that way. But there was no way I was hauling the stroller back up the stairs and facing you again. I moved the office chair. I moved the sideways ladder. I rolled the stroller through. I replaced the office chair and the sideways ladder. Getting into or out of Yom Kippur services should not involve this much physical labor. And it only worked because I happen to be privileged with a body that could do that kind of physical labor that day. Also, apparently I am especially strong when I am angry.

Still furious as I walked home, I began sinking into the deeper layers of this. And I was reminded that one reason there is resistance to making room for fat bodies is that our size is seen as a personal failure. Did you feel the need to somehow punish me for showing up in the only body I had that day? My body is neither an achievement nor a failure, and neither is yours.

However, even if you believe that my fatness is a result of my wrongdoing, Yom Kippur is a particularly telling time to use this as an excuse for not making room for me and not letting me through. Standing with scrolls of Torah in our arms, just before we chant *Kol Nidrei*, the liturgy of Yom Kippur opens with these words:

> With the consent of the Almighty, and the consent of this congregation, in a convocation of the heavenly court, and a convocation of the lower court, we hereby grant permission to pray with transgressors.

Projections of sinfulness onto my body are no excuse for making me feel unwelcome. On Yom Kippur, I do not have to prove that my body is worthy of inclusion. On this day of all days, even if you think fat people are at fault for our fatness—even, indeed especially, if you think we are "transgressors"—today is a day to make space for us.

4

Making Space
Chairing Is Caring

I am having trouble concentrating, struggling to focus on the words in the prayerbook in my hands. The source of my distraction is a biting pain on the outside of each of my thighs, as the arms of the chair in the synagogue sanctuary dig into me where they meet the seat itself. Nothing about this pain is unusual to me. In fact, this experience is so common, so familiar, so seared into my body and my brain, that I can conjure it now, while I sit and write in a much more comfortable seat.

My strategies for dealing with this discomfort are familiar too: shift frequently so that the pain alternates between one leg and then the other rather than both legs at once; sit far forward in the chair so that I am mostly sort of squatting while trying to make it look like this is some kind of highly evolved meditation pose; maximize those moments in the meeting or in the prayer service or at dinner in someone's home when it is even vaguely appropriate to be hovering on the edge of the room rather than sitting. This hovering works best if you can make yourself and others believe that you are doing this because you are just a spiritually unique creature who prefers to stand and maybe wander around a bit.

If I've been invited to a gathering space that is unfamiliar to me, I sometimes arrive early to scope out my seating options. I assess what has been made available and then often go lurking around the premises looking for a chair or a bench or a low table that will actually work for me. Just recently, for a celebratory event at my daughter's elementary school, I found myself dragging a ratty-looking, seemingly forgotten armless chair down the hallway and into the formal assembly hall where I swapped it out for one of the lovely upholstered wooden chairs that were of no use to me.

In most settings in which I find myself, it is clear that no one has given any thought to the potential presence of people who are my size or larger, much less to how to create a space that welcomes our bodies. Lack of proper seating is only one example of failing to make space for fat people, but it is central enough to gatherings of human beings as to be an excellent example of how the fattest among us are systemically excluded. We often use "a seat at the table" as a metaphor for inclusion; there is nothing metaphorical about my seating needs. Anyone claiming to be concerned about fat people could make their claims much more believable by tending to our actual bodies.

Loving the Stranger

Making space for fat bodies need not even require anyone to make much peace with fatness. The *mitzvah* "You must love the stranger, for you were strangers in the land of Egypt" (Deuteronomy 10:19), the most oft-repeated commandment in all of Torah, is a call to see to the needs of people whom we need not feel comfortable with. This *mitzvah* commands us to center those who have been marginalized. However, "center," importantly, does not mean "assimilate."

Too often we try to love those who have been overlooked or pushed aside by trying to make them similar to ourselves. Making space for fat people forces us, I hope, to take seriously the concerns of twentieth-century Jewish philosopher Emmanuel Levinas, who made it clear that the key to loving the stranger was recognizing that "the Other remains . . . infinitely foreign."[1] We can, and we must, take care of one another without minimizing, making light of, or trying to erase our differences or our discomforts with those differences. All of us can actively make more welcoming spaces for fat people no matter how we *feel* about our own or anyone else's body.

The Dissonance of (Un)Welcoming Spaces

A lack of welcome is particularly jarring at gatherings that pride themselves on being spaces of belonging. You may be familiar with the cat memes "If it fits, I sits," which show felines squeezing themselves into boxes—and fish bowls and vases and flower pots—that seem like they would certainly be too small for the creature in question. When it comes to humans, we need to consider the opposite: If we can't sit, we will never feel like we fit. When this basic need goes unmet, true belonging is elusive.

While I dream of an entire world free of anti-fat bias, lack of proper seating creates a deeper wound when it happens at gatherings of family and friends or in synagogues or other community spaces. I may be equally physically uncomfortable in the waiting room of the car repair shop, but I am not facing the same disappointment that I do in a place where I was told I would feel at home. In fact, it is especially in light of how unwelcoming so many human-built spaces are to fat people that I yearn for communal gatherings that I can trust to be places of refuge.

One community I had long admired but never visited used "Come as you are" as their prominent motto. It was in their every email and brochure, and they really meant it; they had built an impressive reputation, in a slow-to-change city, as a prayer space that was truly welcoming to people of all backgrounds. But when I arrived for Shabbat morning services with one very active toddler, I found that the seating was composed mostly of plastic chairs with arms spaced far too close together for me to even contemplate trying to sit in them. In one back corner of the gathering space, there was one partial row of plastic chairs without arms, the kind I have learned to perch on gently, positioning myself in such a way that if the chair breaks I will hopefully fall forward and lower my risk of a head injury.

Theoretically I could squeeze my way back to this part of the room, asking numerous people to stand up to let me by. However, the addition of my toddler made this so impractical as to be impossible. There was no way she was going to be able to stay only in that part of the room. Surely she would want to run around with the other kids, but the configuration of the space meant that I could not both have a seat that (sort of) accommodated me and be able to supervise her.

Once again I found myself hovering off to one side of the room. Once again I felt as if I could never fully arrive. Once again I knew I would hesitate to return to this space.

This distance between our aspiration to create spaces of belonging—inviting people to "come as you are"—and our failure to accommodate bodies of all sizes (and all abilities and all races and all genders and all sexualities) creates a soul-deep disappointment. We want our homes to be welcoming to all we invite in. We want our communal spaces to be houses of worship and gathering, centers of learning and community. We certainly do not want them to be houses of pain and centers of physical discomfort. It is the dissonance of this kind of experience—the promise and expectation of welcome combined with a reality that is the opposite of welcome—that bespeaks the harm done by systemic anti-fatness, a moral injury, in far too many well-meaning spaces.

Uneven Impact

It is important to remember that the fatphobia that goes into constructing human-built spaces does not impact all bodies equally. It is a form of anti-fatness that primarily affects those of us in the largest bodies. Many people in smaller fat bodies, who are negatively impacted by weight stigma in other ways—in terms of their own relationships with their bodies and their interpersonal interactions—may themselves be unaware of these issues of basic access to physical spaces. I am also keenly aware as I write this that I too still have plenty to learn about the different needs of bodies that are larger than mine or those that have different accessibility needs of other kinds.

Those with much more thin privilege than I have, even if they have wrestled with internalized anti-fat bias and then come to a good relationship with their own bodies, may be practicing a form of self-acceptance based on staying within a particular size range or focusing on the things their body can achieve. Body positivity that is conditioned on not being "too fat," on a particular level of athleticism, or on pride that your body has birthed a child is not the kind of embrace of fatness that creates welcoming spaces for all.

Thin privilege is always relative, and raising our own awareness of the needs of those who are larger than we are—as well as those in bodies that are marginalized in other ways than ours—is part of the ongoing practice of allyship that all of us can take on. In other words, the fact that these issues of physical access primarily impact only the largest among us is a reason to center these concerns rather than leaving them as an afterthought in our desire for body liberatory communities. The exclusion of one part of the population always diminishes the community as a whole.

Obstacles to Welcoming

A number of obstacles keep us from being able to set up spaces that are free from this most tangible manifestation of anti-fatness. Thin privilege can keep us from even noticing the needs of fat people. The stigma and shame that too many of us have internalized can also keep us from being able to advocate for or even acknowledge our own needs. Additionally, the many repeated experiences of exclusion can make us reluctant to even show up in communal spaces. When our needs are voiced, we can be met with the idea that the way the space is constructed is "just the way it is"; even those with the power to make change can feel that there are no other options. Finally, there is no getting around the fact that most of us are disinclined to change because fat people are blamed and punished for the needs we have; our fatness is seen as something we have "done to ourselves."

Thin Privilege and Not Noticing

Being unaware of fat people's needs is a hallmark of thin privilege. This was made clear to me in the *sukkah* of a rabbi friend of mine. A *sukkah*—a temporary dwelling erected for the celebration of the fall festival of Sukkot—is meant to be an iffy structure. *Sukkot* are built to let the rain in, to let the stars be visible through the roof, and to last only for a week. There is plenty of *halakhah* (Jewish law) around how *sukkot* are meant to be constructed and what makes a *sukkah* kosher or unkosher. But nowhere is there a requirement that they be as inaccessible as they often are. The particular *sukkah* to which I had been invited for lunch seemed alright. I noticed immediately a chair right by the structure's entrance that I would need to claim for myself, since there was no room for me to squeeze behind others to get into or out of any of the other seats. And I knew I could employ my usual techniques for dealing with the lightweight plastic chair.

In a moment of sacred choreography gone awry, we all stood around the table while our host made *kiddush* (a blessing over wine that marks the sacredness of the holiday). Then, we all sat down together, symbolizing the fulfillment of the commandment of dwelling in the *sukkah*. But one of the legs of our host's plastic chair was over the edge of the low patio, and as she sat down her weight rested on only two of its legs. When the chair broke, thankfully she was fine. She was able to stand right up, and someone quickly got her another chair. This time she sat down securely, looked around at her guests, and said, "Who knew that these chairs were so flimsy?!?"

I felt like someone in a comedy sketch whose hand flies into the air as if in answer to an actual question, only to be quickly pulled back down when realizing that the question was merely rhetorical and that everyone else in attendance was nodding along in agreement with the speaker. I knew that the chair was flimsy, but it was clear from the nodding heads that no one else had previously contemplated this fact.

There are two important aspects to note about her statement in question form. The first is that her rhetorical question shows one of the truest marks of privilege: she literally had not known what every fat person in the world would know at a glance. The flimsiness or sturdiness of the chairs, and by extension the needs of any fat person she might invite into this sacred space, had never occurred to her before, though she had already known me—and hopefully other fat people—personally for years.

The second striking aspect of her rhetorical question is that when she sat on the chair and it broke, she automatically blamed the chair for its flimsiness. Most fat people I know in the same situation would feel at least a passing twinge of shameful self-blame, would be blamed by others, or both. It was nothing short of revelatory for me that she experienced the broken chair as a problem with the chair and not with her body.

Fat People's Internalized Stigma

It is this internalized shame and stigma—this well-learned, knee-jerk self-blame when faced with an unwelcoming space or a broken chair—that keeps too many of us, myself often included, from simply lovingly acknowledging what our needs are and speaking up in order to have those needs met. While it would be wonderful to be able to rely on the allyship of our thinner peers to make change, there is no substitute for advocating for ourselves. However, our ability to do so in any given situation depends on how much internalized stigma we are experiencing in the moment, as well as whatever else is impacting our relative resilience or vulnerability on a given day; no one should double their own suffering by being ashamed that they were not a "good fat activist" when they had a chance to be.

I am often hesitant to urge self-advocacy on people who are in vulnerable situations, where speaking up for ourselves risks a worse outcome than whatever we are initially experiencing. Many of us have spoken up only to be met with insults instead of accommodations. True change will require a combination of fat people speaking up on our own behalf and supporting one another in being able to do so and decision-makers learning to take our needs into account when making choices about spaces and their furnishings.

Oppressive Systemization

One obstacle that often arises when people do advocate for the needs of their own or another's fat body is a defensiveness about the human choices that go into decisions that reinforce anti-fatness. For example, I've lost track of the number of community events where we are all expected to wear T-shirts ordered especially for the event and I have shown up to find that no one ordered a T-shirt in my size. When I question this, even far in advance of the event, I am usually met with the answer that it is impossible to include me because the company they order from just doesn't make shirts in my size. This is always framed as "just the way things are" and never as an issue of purposeful decision-making. The standardization of sizing—whether of shirts or of chairs—is framed as somehow out of human hands, as if these sizes and their relative availability were given to Moses at Mount Sinai right along with the Ten Commandments. But people made choices at every step along the way: the event organizer chose which T-shirt printing company to order from, the printing company chose which clothing manufacturer to get their shirts from, and the clothing manufacturer chose what sizes to make. Anti-fat bias influenced each of these choices in turn; at each point the cost of a T-shirt that would fit me was deemed too high a price to pay for my inclusion.

We used to make clothing to fit people. Now we expect people to fit into certain sizes, and we laud this system as both efficient and economical. Sizes—of people, clothing, chairs—became standardized under the forces of industrialization and mass production. Perhaps this kind of economizing need not be inherently problematic. However, it becomes deeply problematic when standardization is mapped onto marginalizing ideas about who and what is "normal" and "abnormal." Societal ideals of what constitutes an "acceptable" size have gotten narrower just as people (in some populations) have gotten larger. This moralization of sizing then extends to putting the blame for not fitting on those whom we have, as a society, chosen to exclude. All of this would seem to be easily reversible: human decisions can simply be made differently. But when human choices accrete into systems, we have a tendency to pretend there is nothing we can do about it because this is "just the way the world is."

In my parenting, I have also been known to resort to the tactic of avoiding responsibility by blaming the system or the technology. My children's electronic devices are set to automatically turn off at a particular time in the evening. This allows me to sympathize with them about how hard it is when the tablet turns off—eschewing the truth that I am the one who picked the time for the tablet to turn off. This method has resulted in far fewer tears around our house. So I understand the draw to saying, "It wasn't me; it was the machine." But I also see very clearly how it is a way of quashing resistance to injustice, silencing those who are crying out against unfairness.

Exclusionary systems created by human choices become enshrined as "just the way things are." When they align with larger forces of oppression, these systems are, ultimately, dehumanizing: they value the smooth running of the system more than they value human experiences and, ultimately, human lives. In making space for fat people, we have a unique opportunity to make our families and our communities bastions of opposition to this dehumanization.

People come in all sizes; human size is an unbroken continuum of diversity. Indeed, the diversity of Creation is seen as a testament to God's greatness, as when the psalmist sings in praise, "How manifold are Your creations, YHVH! You have made them all with wisdom" (Psalm 104:24). Born to this wide and wild diversity, it is we humans who make decisions, conscious or otherwise, to demarcate and divide. Imagine if our choices about chairs reflected a desire to honor and celebrate the physical diversity of humanity.

Blaming and Punishing Fat People

Beneath the obstacles of fat people's needs going unnoticed, our own internalized stigma, the impact of repeated harm, and the systemization of our oppression lies this painful cultural bedrock: fat people are blamed for the biases we face. When our fatness is seen as our fault, our marginalization is constructed as completely justified. Beyond both the scientific debate and the societal back-and-forth about what combination of genetics, social determinants, individual choices, and environmental factors leads a person to have any particular body size is this moral truth: human beings deserve to have their physical needs met regardless of the cause of those needs. Questions of fault have no place in our calculations of who deserves to take up their own space.

Refuge from Repeated Harm

Of course, there is nothing uniquely Jewish about being unwelcoming to larger bodies. It is important that we understand that fat people arrive in Jewish spaces—from our own homes to larger centers of community gathering—from a wider world that is not welcoming either. We show up in Jewish spaces wounded from our experiences both within the community and beyond. In too many educational settings and entertainment venues, we face fixed seating that was not built with our bodies in mind. And as we have already covered, the medical world is even more harmful: from hospital gowns that do not fit to MRI machines and other equipment that either cannot accommodate larger bodies at all or cannot be used to accurately measure what they are meant to measure.

Change needs to happen in these areas as well. But imagine what a pleasure and a source of healing it would be to know that, in an unwelcoming world, at least there was a space for me in my Jewish community. I dream of a world in which making space for actual fat people's actual bodies is centered as a Jewish value. Imagine what our religious and spiritual experiences could look like if our synagogues and schools and summer camps were strongholds of belonging for all bodies.

Recognizing Need

What might our lives look like if we made decisions about the construction, furnishing, and arrangement of spaces with the needs of fat people in mind? You cannot assess a fat person's health or "lifestyle choices" just by looking at them. But do you know what we could get much better at knowing just by looking? Whether the fat person in front of you might need a chair that is sturdier or wider than the one you were planning on offering them.

Too often, fat people are hyper-visible while our needs are rendered completely invisible. When I walk into a room, I feel like the size of my butt and the size of the chairs available are easy to assess. Almost any person my size can tell stories about the unwanted attention we are subject to and the obviousness with which our size is noticed and noticeable. However, in "polite company," noticing someone's size is considered rude. While in both cases there is an assumption that my size is or ought to be seen as shameful, the veneer of politeness renders a strange split-screen reality in which my size is simultaneously obvious and invisible.

I recently went to an outdoor café here in Jerusalem and decided I would advocate for myself. I noticed that there were plenty of armless chairs inside the café but that none of the patio seating would fit me. So, when the staff person who seated us asked if the outdoor table he was indicating would work for us, I said, "It's perfect, but I would like a chair that fits me better." He looked at me like he could not imagine what I was asking for. I reviewed my Hebrew in my head, but no, I was being perfectly clear: I needed a different chair. Finally, instead of trying to make my actual need understood, I simply pointed to the chair I wanted and asked if we could use that one instead. He got me the chair but continued to seem baffled by my request.

My size is notable, my fatness obvious, to anyone who sees me. Why are my needs not equally obvious? I have strong evidence, in the form of decades of both "well-meaning" advice and plain old street harassment, that makes it clear that other people can tell that I am fat. This makes the bafflement that I might have space-related needs feel downright Kafkaesque or like a form of gaslighting: either I am denying reality or you are.

By contrast, when people are primed to be attentive to fat people's needs, assessing those needs can be relatively straightforward, even when the fat person in question is not right in front of you. My parents' synagogue hosts a Sunday morning Alcoholics Anonymous meeting. Volunteers from the synagogue set up the room in advance and then rearrange everything again afterward. For a couple of weeks in a row, my parents noticed that after the meeting they came in to find a broken folding chair. That was all the proof they needed that the chairs they were providing were not accommodating to at least one anonymous attendee. They went out and bought a few sturdier chairs and never dealt with a broken chair again.

One can imagine this scenario playing out quite differently. Synagogue members could have seen those same broken chairs and immediately been angry with the group they were claiming to welcome: "We let you use our space and you break our community's property?!?" Indeed, there were those voices that did call for disinviting the group. But a shift in attitude allows us to realize that if we claim to be welcoming, then it is on us to meet people's physical needs. The failure here lies not with the chair breaker but with those who did not offer a sufficiently sturdy chair in the first place.

We may think of it as impolite to talk about people's bodies. But we do need to notice and talk about our bodies' needs. Too often we worry too much about "impoliteness" while not worrying enough about the underlying beliefs, worldviews, and oppressive structures that create unequal access in the first place. Concerns about politeness reinforce the idea that there is something shameful about our bodies' basic needs, something that ought to be embarrassing about being fat.

Some fat people may indeed be embarrassed by their own needs. The shame caused by internalized bias means that not every fat person—or any fat person all the time—can even identify, articulate, or ask for what we need. I am still growing in my ability to make sure in advance that my body will be accommodated when I arrive in a new space to teach or lead prayer. I try to have compassion on myself for choosing so often to hover at the back of the room, being "eccentric" instead of asking for my needs to be met. It is tiring to always have to advocate for my needs in the face of others' refusal to even acknowledge my body. This drain on fat people's energy should not be underestimated.

A truly diverse community will contain all kinds of bodies with all kinds of needs. Rarely is a solution truly "one size fits all." For example, as of this writing, I am someone who is able to stand up from a chair without needing arms to help me up. But trying to be welcoming to fat people by simply having all the chairs be armless would create an accessibility problem for people of various sizes who do rely on a chair's arms to help themselves up or down. And the widest possible array of chairs will not do fat people any good if the configuration of the space itself is inaccessible: the right kind of chairs are useless if they, or the tables in a room, are spaced too closely together for me to get through. A community committed to making space for bodies of all sizes can choose to make at least some of its seating—not to mention the path to the exit—accessible and to announce its availability in advance.

The changes we need to make are both structural and cultural. Attending to the needs of fat people also means raising the consciousness of the community about how the space is used. The presence of chairs that are accessible to a particular kind of body is not enough if those chairs are constantly occupied by people who do not need them. One synagogue I attended regularly for some time had a good combination of chairs with and without arms, all thoughtfully arranged in the sanctuary. But in all my years of attendance, if I walked into that space and all of the armless chairs were taken, not once did someone who could have just as easily sat in a chair with arms offer me their armless chair. Welcoming people of all sizes must still start with a willingness to take notice of our actual bodies and to recognize fat bodies' needs.

Of course, our needs also extend beyond chairs. We need towels and robes at the *mikveh* (ritual bath) that let us know we belong in this space where we are literally naked and at our most vulnerable. A lack of the right sizes of life jackets and other gear at summer camps not only is harmful psychologically to larger kids but can create a safety hazard. And I still long for the day when the T-shirts that everyone is expected to wear on "Mitzvah Day" or for some other community event are actually ordered in sizes that let fat people know that this event is for us too.

Centering Fat People's Experiences

A call for fat-inclusive physical spaces focuses our attention on the needs of the largest among us. It calls us to center those who are the most marginalized, to care for the "strangest" stranger. As Rabbi Rachel Grant Meyer pointed out to me, we cannot do the rest of the work of uprooting anti-fatness if we literally cannot get people seated at the table. For this reason, while some forms of fatphobia can impact people of all sizes, it is important that we actively refrain from shying away from the needs of the fattest among us.

Talking about fatness, not to mention real live fat people, makes many of us uncomfortable. It is too easy to let conversations about weight stigma drift into the more comfortable and diffuse framings of self-love and "body positivity." However, this drift reinforces the exclusion of actual fat people. Allowing the constructions of our spaces to be a touchstone in any conversation about body liberation can help us stay focused on ensuring that we are making room for the largest among us.

Make Me a Sanctuary

Every gathering has the potential to create a sacred space that recognizes all people as created in the image of the Divine. While leading the people through the wilderness on the journey from Narrowness to freedom, Moses receives instructions from God to build a *mishkan* (tabernacle). The root of *mishkan* is ש-כ-ן—the same root as

Shekhinah, the aspect of the Divine that in older rabbinic texts is the most immanent or closest to us as humans. In later Jewish mysticism, the Shekhinah is the Divine feminine. The *mishkan* is a space in which God's presence dwells.

Moses is told, "Let them make me a sanctuary, that I may dwell among them" (Exodus 25:8). The "them" of this verse does not refer to an elite privileged "in crowd" but to the whole people, to all of us together. We must imagine that, had God wanted it this way, the *mishkan* could have simply floated down from the heavens as a divine prefab. Instead, the text makes clear the humanness and earthliness employed in the making of this first sacred space. It names those who are called upon to be in charge of this work and also allows for everyone else to participate as well. While Betzalel is singled out to lead the *mishkan*'s construction (Exodus 35:30–34), we are also told specifically about women who were skilled in weaving, as well as the invitation to everyone to contribute to the building of this sacred space in whatever ways they are able (Exodus 35:25–29). While some people are in charge of making the big decisions, every one of us is expected to contribute to the project. I would also like to imagine into our Torah the voices of those who took on the role of pointing out when bad choices were being made—choices that would keep the space from living up to its ideal.

Unlike the folks who built the *mishkan*, we do not have the same divinely ordained, detailed instructions about how to make our own spaces accommodating to God and people alike. The humanness of the construction of our communal lives means that we can create spaces into which the worst of systemic oppressions creep or spaces where all bodies belong. The choices, the many, many choices, are right there in our own hands. And when we notice that a given space is unwelcoming, we also have it in our own hands to rebuild. Sometimes this is as simple as creating a different arrangement of the furniture we already have, and sometimes it means literally tearing down walls.

From its beginnings as a sacrificial setup in the desert, the ideal of human-made sacred spaces extends to all of our gathering places: our homes themselves are described as *mikdash me'at* (a sanctuary in miniature). And in one soaringly hopeful prophetic vision, God describes the sacred space of our wildest dreams, saying, "My House shall be called a house of prayer for all peoples" (Isaiah 56:7). Everywhere we invite the Divine to dwell is meant to have space for the vast diversity of humanity to be welcomed as well.

We are talking about making basic changes to objects of plastic, wood, and metal. Yet when we truly make space for fat people, our gatherings—whether meeting for coffee, hosting a Shabbat dinner, or praying together in a formal synagogue setting—can create sacred spaces, with the potential to embody divinity itself.

In the Zohar, the central text of Jewish mysticism that appeared in Spain in the late thirteenth century, Shekhinah is also referred to as *Knesset Yisrael* (Assembly of Israel). In other words, not only does Shekhinah follow us in our people's wanderings and dwell within and among us wherever we make space for Her, but our fullest, most inclusive gatherings actually constitute the Divine Presence itself. And the converse is also true: our failures to create gatherings that make space for all of us diminish the Shekhinah Herself. God's presence cannot fully exist in our midst when that midst has not made room for fat people.

For Our Sake the World Was Created

In a Fat Torah community gathering, one participant made the heartbreaking statement, "This world just wasn't made for us." How painful, to move through the world with nowhere that fits us, no space for us to be our own human selves. Jewish tradition offers a precise antidote to this experience and a very different vision of how things ought to be. The Mishnah we learned in chapter 2 (Sanhedrin 4:5) about death penalty cases and human worth ends with a truly striking statement. After teaching about each person's uniqueness and the infinite value of every human being, it concludes that it is incumbent on all of us, created in the image of the Divine, to boldly lay claim to the statement "For my sake the world was created."

Human choices shape our physical environments into twisted spaces infused with anti-fatness. But our existential place in this world remains untouched. Holding fast to the fullness of fat people's humanity by seeing to our basic physical needs is an antidote to a society that regularly ignores, denigrates, and mistreats us. We can help one another recover the knowing that the world was created for each and every one of us. We can let our gatherings be microcosms of this ultimate belonging.

To the rabbi whose congregants were upset about gaining weight

It was so good to speak with you about the possibility of bringing a Fat Torah workshop to your community. I enjoyed hearing about how devoted your congregation is to social justice, and I love the idea of expanding their circle of concern to include confronting anti-fat bias.

However, I've been mulling over one thing that I said to you, and I want to come back to it. You mentioned that one impetus for inviting me to teach was that a number of congregants had reached out to you because they were struggling with having gained weight during COVID-19 lockdowns and other pandemic-related disruptions to their bodies and their routines. You wondered if I might have some insights on how to respond to them.

In a moment of unguarded collegiality I blurted out, "Yes, it does suck to lose privilege, doesn't it?" I could immediately see on your face, even on Zoom, that what I had said was shocking and unhelpful. Though our conversation had been steeped in singing your community's praises in the realm of social justice, my use of a strictly social justice framing in response to the pain of your community members was, in retrospect, callous and uncaring. A delicious "zinger" born of my own pain, it worked perfectly well as an expression of my anger but was unlikely to be of any benefit to either you or your congregants. I would never have said such a thing to congregants or students of my own who were bringing me their very real pain.

Here is what I hope I could have said instead: Change is hard. Having a body is frightening. Any change in our body can be deeply unsettling, causing us to become unfamiliar to ourselves. Our whole sense of who we are can be disrupted when our bodies go from a size that we believe is "healthy" to a size that everyone tells us is "unhealthy"—whether or not either of these assessments is objectively true. And it is not only our own internal beliefs at play here. How are people meant to experience these physical changes when their bodies are changing in ways that public health experts are warning make us more vulnerable to severe illness or death? And how can they possibly separate these health-related concerns from broader fears of their newfound fatness making them vulnerable to plain old anti-fat bullying? In a world where fat bodies are so widely and uncontestedly denigrated, such fears are completely realistic.

So, yes, I would hope that I would be able to respond to your congregants with an abundance of patience and compassion. At the same time, I also have compassion for myself for responding as flippantly as I did. I am a fat woman who was just as fat the day before COVID-19 was discovered as I was on the day that we spoke. While I would like to imagine that I have been training my entire life for just these moments, it still hurts to hear that people have reached out to you because they are pained and terrified that their bodies are coming to more closely resemble mine. And where was their concern about the denigration of bodies like mine before they themselves gained weight?

On an intellectual level, I believe that your congregants' healing and mine are woven together. And I feel this, too, deep down at the soul level, where all distinctions and labels and gradations and human systems melt away. But right here in the middle where my heart is, where my guts are, where my whole body is, it is harder in difficult moments to find my love and compassion for them. It is not impossible, but it is hard.

While I could certainly have framed it more gently, I stand by my instinct that there *is* something to be gained by understanding at least some of your congregants' pain as the pain of losing privilege. Compassionately framed for people who are open to hearing it, this kind of understanding allows us to begin unlearning our own anti-fatness and cultivating deeper care for our own and everyone's bodies. Not only does this allow us to take part in dismantling the scourge of anti-fatness in society as a whole, it also benefits each of us individually: understanding our personal pain as part of a larger system can help us feel less alone.

My own ongoing healing necessitates finding and expressing compassion for people who are uncomfortable in their newly fat bodies—usually still much smaller than my own—in ways that do not reinforce my own degradation and do not capitulate to fat hatred. While I aspire to help you care for the members of your community, I am steadfastly committed to doing so in a fat-embracing way.

5

As We Love Ourselves

The size of a butt and the size of a seat are objectively measurable. By contrast, our feelings about bodies and fatness—our own and others'—are immeasurably more subjective. Similarly, the changes we can all advocate for in order to make physical space for fat people are also relatively straightforward—simple, though not easy. Once we enter the tangle of how we each relate to our own bodies and how we speak about fatness, both harm and healing become much less clear.

The story that begins this book—about the Chanukah party that launched Fat Torah and the song leader who said, "Let's all get back to dancing, unless you've gotten too fat from those *sufganiyot*"—is one that I have by now told dozens if not hundreds of times. Much more than once, a listener has heard this story, squinched up their face sympathetically, and said, "Oh . . . and you took that *personally*." For them, the problem with this incident is my own sensitivity, my own tendency toward hearing any degradation of fatness as a statement about my own body.

While I, like most people my size, have certainly been subjected to plenty of explicit judgments of my own body, most of the anti-fat speech that I am exposed to multiple times every day comes in the form of people making statements—or posting memes or cracking jokes or soliciting my input—either about their own bodies or about fatness more generally. More often than not, this hurts me. I am pained by the endless, casual conversations that imagine weight loss as unconditionally desirable. I have a deep aversion to hearing individuals complaining about weight gain or celebrating weight loss. And I have never heard or seen a "fat joke" that did not make me cringe.

I am not judging anyone's intentions in saying such things. I am not denying anyone else's very real pain when they put down their own bodies. I do not want to police anyone's speech. But I do want to share how I am impacted when people denigrate their own bodies or fatness in general. I am measuring harm using my own feelings as a sensor. That, of course, has its limits, but I have grown to trust my heart when it tells me that something hurts. I know that the meanings I make of the incidents I am sharing here do not speak for everyone; I also know that I am far from alone.

After one doctor's visit, in which I felt my provider was letting her feelings about her body get in the way of providing me with decent care, I wrote:

I see your hatred of your own body projected
on the broad screen that is my chest.
I am infected
by your fear.

Early on in their wanderings in the wilderness, the Children of Israel must deal with a similar infection. Having made their way out of the narrowness of slavery, walked on dry land across a sea that parted for them, and received Torah at Mount Sinai, the people come to the Wilderness of Paran from which they are poised to enter the Promised Land (Numbers 12:16). At this point, they face a body image problem of biblical proportions.

At God's command, Moses had sent scouts to case the Promised Land and assess the people's prospects for moving in. Among other things, Moses wants to know if the land is fat enough to sustain them (Numbers 13:20). The twelve scouts return after forty days and report that the land is indeed flowing with milk and honey. Unfortunately, some of the scouts are afraid that their bid to enter the land will fail due to the overwhelming size and strength of the current inhabitants. When one of the scouts, Caleb, tries to counter this concern, the others lie and say that the land is full of giants. "We were like grasshoppers in our own eyes," they cry, "and so we appeared to them" (Numbers 13:33).

Perceiving themselves as puny grasshoppers, they devalue and underestimate themselves, their whole people, and even God Godself. Yet it is not their negative perceptions of their bodies themselves that prove problematic. All of us, biblical spies and otherwise, are entitled to feel everything we ever feel. Catastrophe is created not by their feelings but by how they choose to speak about those feelings. It is the words they use in describing their sense of physical inadequacy that infect nearly the entire community.

As a consequence of this widespread body panic, God decides that the people will continue their wandering in the wilderness for another forty years. Once we start dealing with feelings about our own bodies and especially how we choose to speak about those feelings, we too are no longer on an easy path right from narrowness into the promised land of fat freedom for all. We too are twisting and turning our way through the wilderness.

Having a Body

Whether in the public eye of a high-pressured scouting mission or in the privacy of our own bedrooms, we are allowed to feel any way we feel about our bodies. A body is a strange companion on a soul's journey through life. Our relationships with our own bodies—as they constantly both grow and age—can be expected to change daily, if not hourly, as we move in them through different social contexts, roles, life stages, illnesses, and other changes.

I remember spotting the very first freckle to emerge on the back of my daughter's little neck. She was not quite one and a half that summer when the sun tickled the melanin in that particular handful of cells. Tears came to my eyes as I recognized this as one tiny instance of the innumerable ways that life would keep impacting her precious body and her relationship with it.

My relationship with my own body and with my fatness continues to grow and change in interaction both with the anti-fatness around me and within me and with my ongoing practice of fat acceptance. Pregnancies, perimenopause, and a badly broken ankle are just a few of the body-changing experiences of my past decade. Each has offered new challenges around acceptance and new opportunities for refinding joy. The moments of feeling at home in my own skin feel like daily miracles.

People of all sizes can suffer from negative perceptions of their bodies and of fatness. At the same time, our actual size positions us in a particular relationship to thin privilege and to societal anti-fatness, regardless of how we feel about ourselves in any given moment. My own most positive feelings about my fat body have yet to manifest an accommodating chair, nor can they protect me from discrimination in hiring or incompetence in healthcare. Conversely, a relatively thin person can have a terribly painful view of their own body—with or without having a diagnosed and potentially deadly eating disorder—while simultaneously enjoying the obvious privileges of being able to walk into any clothing store and find something that fits them or to show up at a job interview without their size being judged as disqualifying.

I do not want to understate the torturous state of body hatred and dissatisfaction that too many people of all sizes can face, whether in small moments or as an insidious constant. Entire industries thrive on implanting and maintaining in us the belief that our bodies are wrong in ways large and small. Being honest with ourselves about our feelings toward our bodies is certainly important, but acknowledging what we feel and speaking those feelings aloud are, or ought to be, not the same thing.

Power of Speech

From one perspective, it would be ideal if, as listeners, we were all skilled at easily discerning that what another person says about their body, and its real or perceived fatness, has nothing to do with our own bodies. Just the other day, a friend earnestly told me that I should hear her expression of her desire to lose weight purely as a statement about her own personal preferences. If I have long hair and she wants hers short, I need not hear her aesthetic choice as having any connection whatsoever to my own style.

Theoretically, I need not hear someone's judgment of themselves as a judgment of my own fatness. But this highly individuating approach frames a desire not to be fat as somehow separable from our culture's pervasive anti-fatness; it is not. Often the most painfully anti-fat speech I hear are expressions of body hatred spoken by people who are almost always smaller than I am. I do not know how to hear the anti-fatness that thinner people direct at their own bodies as anything other than a hatred of fatness and fat people.

The ability to differentiate and not take personally what someone else says about themselves is certainly vital for therapists, teachers, clergy, and caregivers of all sorts. Plenty of fat people have also told me that they simply do not share my own sensitivity around this; I have no reason not to believe them. However, when we expect this kind of differentiation from all of us, all the time, we risk slipping into victim blaming, putting the burden of pushing back against the voices of anti-fatness solely on the listener. Jewish tradition urges us to not be too quick to absolve ourselves, as speakers, of the duty to be mindful of our speech and the damage it can cause, especially to people in bodies more marginalized than our own.

Judaism recognizes the potential of speech as a great force for both creativity and destruction. Recalling the very beginning of Torah in which reality is created through divine speech, our morning prayers praise "The One who spoke and the world came to be." Concerned with the destructive power of human words, Talmud (BT Arakhin 15b) wrestles with the verse "Death and life are in the hand of the tongue" (Proverbs 18:21). Rabbi Ḥama is curious about this biblical image of the tongue having a hand. He says that the verse means that "just as a hand can kill so too a tongue can kill." And while a hand can only kill from close by, Rabbi Ḥama brings a different verse about how the "tongue is a sharpened arrow" (Jeremiah 9:7) to emphasize that—like an arrow shot from a bow—our speech can do great harm even from a significant distance.

Feeling Fat

When I was contacted by a rabbi who wondered whether Fat Torah might collaborate with his organization, I was initially enthusiastic about the possibility. My enthusiasm immediately fizzled though when he said that he was especially interested in Fat Torah because he understands what fat people experience because he sometimes "feels fat." The whole concept of "feeling fat" is steeped in anti-fat bias. Fatness is not a feeling; it is simply one aspect of an awe-inspiring variety of human forms.

I experienced this attempt at finding common ground as jarring. He was equating how he *feels* about his body with how others *act* toward me because of my body. What I heard in his claim was basically that he knows how it feels for my fatness to be rejected because he himself also rejects fatness. While I wish him healing in his relationship with his own body, his words make him at least as much a perpetrator of anti-fatness as its victim.

When people say they "feel fat," they are expressing deep discomfort with fatness, as well as fears of their bodies becoming more like mine. Knowing what it feels like to hate my own body, I would not wish such a thing on this rabbi or on anyone else. And I do have deep compassion for anyone who hates themselves. At the same time, it takes a mighty effort on my part to keep his rejection of fatness from impacting the hard-won love and acceptance with which I treat my own fat body. I am challenged by the resentment that can well up in me at having to do so much emotional labor just to have one supposedly collegial conversation.

This is not only about the particular expression "feeling fat." I have noticed a wider tendency for all sorts of people—most of them significantly thinner than I am—to want to share their negative body image issues with me. This happens especially when I am asked what my work is and I tell them about Fat Torah; even though I describe the work as using Jewish tradition to confront anti-fatness, the assumption seems to be that when I say "confronting anti-fatness" I mean that I am ashamed of or uncomfortable with my own fat body and that I am inviting them to share their own discomfort with their (generally not as fat) bodies.

When someone looks at my body, or knows that I describe myself as fat, and then assumes that I am dissatisfied with my fatness, they are projecting their own anti-fatness onto me. The assumption that mutual body hatred is something that even complete strangers share in common makes shared rejection of fatness an overused casual conversation starter. The hope seems to be that we can use self-rejection to get closer to one another. Instead, the revelation that you are dissatisfied with your body almost always pushes me away.

Sharing Our Journeys

When I shared the news that my book chapter "Your Belly Is a Heap of Wheat"[1] had been published, a dear teacher of mine wrote to congratulate me. The chapter contains a number of examples of anti-fatness that I have experienced personally. In the email, in addition to his words of congratulation for having my work in print, my teacher also responded to my experiences of anti-fat bias with the two-word sentence "Painful stories."

Receiving this supposed sympathy enraged me. So much so that for weeks afterward, I found myself listening over and over again to Sinead O'Connor singing "Black Boys on Mopeds" with its searing opening words decrying what O'Connor saw as the two-facedness of the Conservative British prime minister's response to the killing of Chinese protestors in Tiananmen Square in 1989:

> *Margaret Thatcher on TV*
> *shocked by the deaths that took place in Beijing.*
> *It seems strange that she should be offended.*
> *The same orders are given by her.*

The scale of the violence is clearly different. Yet it still "seems strange" to me that my teacher "should be offended" by my stories of people shooting down fatness in my presence when I have so often heard him speak publicly about wanting to lose weight in ways that continually reinforce a broader anti-fatness. Undoubtedly, it is my love and admiration for my teacher that makes me particularly hurt by what I can only experience as hypocrisy.

I deeply believe that anyone who wants to pursue weight loss is "allowed" to do so; every human being has the right to make this choice for their own body. No one needs to seek my permission or try to convince me that I should give them my approval because they want to lose weight for health reasons. I truly do not care, and definitely do not want to hear, why anyone wants to lose weight. I do not value the pursuit of weight loss for health reasons any more or any less than I value it for reasons of aesthetics, a wish to no longer be the target of anti-fat bias, or a plain old desire for conformity. Of course, part of me wishes I could forcibly remove every single person from the idolatry of diet culture in the same way well-meaning relatives might want to yank a loved one out of a cult. But I truly do value body autonomy.

My teacher is, of course, not alone. Talking about dieting publicly is ubiquitous and nearly inescapable in our culture. I have heard of more than one rabbi who thought it would be a good idea to "share their weight-loss journey" in the form of an actual sermon in front of their entire congregation. In a Jewish context, this is sometimes framed as *teshuva* (repentance or turning away from wrongdoing), and the audience—whether that audience consists of family members, a circle of friends, a community, or an online following—is being asked to provide the dieter with "accountability" by witnessing either their "success" or their "failure." If losing weight is *teshuva*, the only logical conclusion is that gaining weight, or staying fat, is sinful.

By itself, it is problematic to speak about personal choices around pursuing weight loss in ways that cast shame on others. When people make this choice and then claim to be pained by my stories about encounters with anti-fatness, it is hard for me to trust that they actually care about me. I cannot trust you to embrace my fatness while rejecting your own. I cannot trust that you love me when you do not love yourself. I cannot believe that you understand my pain when you continue to denigrate your own body.

Too frequently I encounter people who express sadness about my pain while not recognizing the pain in their judgments of their own bodies. As we learn in Talmud (BT Berakhot 28a) our tradition has mixed feelings about the exacting expectation that all of us live with "our insides like our outsides" all the time. I am not here to demand a particular level of fat acceptance, at any given moment, from anyone, myself included. Still, my wish would be that true caring would come from caring, that caring for another would be an outgrowth of caring for oneself. When someone rejects their own body, it makes their professed love for mine untrustworthy, suspect.

Still, I do think there are things we can do to care for one another even if we do not care for ourselves. Being mindful of our speech is a stopgap measure that can keep us from the worst consequences of this mismatch between our rejection of our bodies and our desire to love the bodies of others. Many parents I know, for example, wrestle with how to avoid passing on their negative feelings about their bodies to their children. It feels punitive to expect people to perfectly "cure" their relationship with their own body before becoming parents lest it negatively impact their children. Rather, the key to interrupting this intergenerational anti-fatness is being conscious of what we *say* to our children as well as what we say about our own bodies or bodies in general anywhere in our children's earshot.

False Positives

Another problematic way that people talk about their own bodies is a particular form of "body positivity" that is predicated on paying less attention to what our bodies look like by emphasizing instead what our bodies are capable of. I ordered a pair of shoes a couple of years ago and saw that I could add a cute little fanny pack to my order for a steeply discounted price. I was quite amused when it arrived to see that the fanny pack included a patch that read, "My body took me here." The implication was that at the top of a mountain, or at the end of whatever other physical feat I had achieved, my fanny pack would remind me to be proud of my body for what it could do. I immediately began imagining other places my body could also take me, chuckling to myself at the thought of strapping on this fanny pack in a hospital bed or even getting someone to make sure I could be buried with it when I die. Surely, my body can take me to those places as well and be no less worthy of basic human dignity. Acceptance of the body that is conditioned on accomplishment is deeply ableist and often anti-fat as well. It tells us that our fat bodies are only acceptable if they can achieve certain fitness goals.

We see another variant on this conditional acceptance of the body in people who claim that they are proud, or at least not ashamed, of how their fat bellies look because their belly became fat while they were "growing a child." The fat belly is seen as a price that was paid for parenthood. In addition to reinforcing the idea that bearing a child is a superior way of becoming a parent, what does this way of speaking about fat bellies imply for people whose bellies got fat though they miscarried or as a consequence of unsuccessful fertility treatments or for some other reason having nothing whatsoever to do with childbearing? When pregnant people in the various online parenting communities I participate in complain about their struggles in accepting their pregnancy-related weight gain and advice pours in about how to accept this "valid"—and, they hope, temporary—form of fatness, I always want to chime in, "Have you tried being less fat hating generally and then letting that naturally extend to your own body as well?"

Everyday Anti-Fatness

Yet anti-fatness perfuses every corner of society, and anti-fat speech is nearly inescapable. Even people who are not speaking specifically of their own bodies can still spread this infection in how they talk about fatness more generally. I ran into another dear teacher of mine after we had not seen one another for some time. He asked what kind of work I was doing these days, and I decided to tell him about Fat Torah even though I know that simply hearing the word "fat" without some kind of warning can be jarring for most people.

I was reminded of a story I had heard from Nadav Schwartz, an activist working at the junction of Orthodoxy and queerness in

Israel. He was in his hometown and ran into a teacher of his from his Orthodox high school. The rabbi asked him what he was doing these days, and he said he was working with *homo'im dati'im* (Orthodox queer folks). But his teacher, presumably never imagining that there could be such a thing, heard "*omanim dati'im*" (Orthodox artists). This left Nadav, once he understood his teacher's "mishearing," the choice of whether to reassert that he was indeed working with people who were queer and Orthodox or to let it go. And that was how he found himself yelling, "*Homo'im! Homo'im!*" (Gays! Gays!) on the street of the Orthodox neighborhood in which he grew up.

My own teacher is a very compassionate person, and I trust that he cares about me personally. So even though I had never discussed my fat activism with him before, I knew I could risk it. When I told him the story about the Chanukah party and I got to the punch line about getting too fat to dance, he started to cry, right there in public. Clearly he did not feel that this was a case of me taking things too personally and was genuinely pained to know that people could speak so cruelly about fat bodies in the presence of my fat body.

I have no doubt that he was truly hurt to know that I had been hurt, but I also, once again, found it "strange that he should be offended" to such an extent that he was moved to tears. I know him to be someone who frequently, "jokingly," uses fatness and dieting as metaphors in his classroom. I understand how it can be helpful to use examples from contemporary society to illustrate points being drawn out from ancient texts. Unfortunately, when those examples are steeped in diet culture and anti-fatness, along with other systemic oppressions, they risk further marginalizing students who are already dealing with more than enough stigma. He was understandably taken aback by the blatant interpersonal anti-fatness I was reporting but somehow could not see how he was continuing to perpetuate and support bias in more pervasive subtle forms.

I did not point out this discrepancy to my teacher. In failing to speak up, I felt as if I had missed an opportunity with biblical resonances. "If I am pleasing to you," begs Queen Esther, "let dispatches be written rescinding those that were written by Haman . . . to annihilate the Jews throughout the king's provinces" (Esther 8:5). Here was my chance to play Queen Esther and to leverage my teacher's love for me personally to implore him to save my fat people. I wish I had entreated my teacher to use his sadness at how I was treated to make the "provinces" of his classroom into spaces free from the harm of anti-fatness.

The use of tropes steeped in diet culture and anti-fatness abounds in nearly every communal space in which I find myself. One Shabbat morning, a congregant brings a back brace to lend to a fellow community member. Trying it on at the back of the synagogue sanctuary, where I am supervising my cavorting children, the two community members have a good laugh together about how the back brace is also so "slimming" that maybe the borrower does not "have to lose his belly" after all.

On another Shabbat morning, a family has provided a truly lavish spread for all to enjoy in celebration of an upcoming wedding. Looking at the wide variety of delicious foods, one community member turns to another whom he has never met before and says, "You know what they say, 'Eat the protein and leave the carbs for the *goyim* (non-Jews).'" I have never witnessed a more striking mash-up of diet culture and Borscht Belt xenophobia. The train of thought seems to be that eating carbohydrates causes fatness, which is something we should only wish on our "enemies."

Silence

It is completely daunting to try to imagine how we might stem the torrent of anti-fat speech that spews forth from so many mouths. When people ask me how they might begin to make changes around how people speak about fatness in their community, I tend to stick to one challenging but tightly focused goal: stop complimenting weight loss. When we see someone who has lost weight, many people have an almost knee-jerk urge to offer some form of congratulations. When we do so, we do not really know what we are complimenting. Perhaps this person has lost weight unintentionally due to illness or grief. Maybe we are actually complimenting, and encouraging, an eating disorder. Even if the weight loss has been intentional, we are letting this person know that we were judging their previous higher weight. Since intentional weight loss is rarely sustained, we are also letting them know that we will once again be negatively assessing their bodies when they regain the weight they have lost. And we are also, always, letting everyone in earshot know that we believe it is inherently better to be thin than to be fat.

A corollary to the respect given to the power of speech in Judaism is the respect given to our abilities to simply hold our tongues when the moment calls for silence. "Silence," Rabbi Akiva insists, "is a fence to wisdom" (Pirkei Avot 3:13). Allowing a thought that has arisen to remain unspoken affords us a precious opportunity to reflect on the relative benefits and risks of sharing that thought aloud. Sometimes saying nothing can prevent great harm.

Rebuke and Healing

In nearly all the incidents I have recounted here in which I was hurt by anti-fat speech, and the hypocrisies surrounding it, I did not speak up in the moment. I want to encourage more speaking up by reminding myself that Jewish tradition offers a model of rebuke as a key component of loving relationships. It is a *mitzvah*, an obligation, to speak up when something is not right and to caringly admonish those who are perpetrating harm.

Two verses in Torah speak both to this obligation and to its challenges. The most famous words of these verses are "Love your neighbor as yourself" (Leviticus 19:18). But the words that immediately precede these in the text lend a deep richness to this popular motto. The previous verse says, "You shall not hate your kinsfolk in your heart. Reprove your kindred and incur no guilt on their account" (Leviticus 19:17). These two verses together make a number of connections between love and rebuke.

First, they imply that true reprobation—letting someone know that they have missed the mark—happens only in the context of a loving relationship. "You shall not hate" comes first and is then followed by the call to rebuke. Second, we can read here that, in fact, correcting one another is part of loving one another, when that rebuke can be offered lovingly.

Third, our tradition offers different readings of what it means to *incur no guilt on their account*. Some interpret this to mean that if we do not rebuke our loved ones, we remain complicit in their wrongdoing. In other words, by not pushing back against anti-fatness in someone else's speech, I make it seem as if I agree with their stigmatizing words.

Others say that the guilt we ourselves could incur in biting our tongues and not speaking up is that we are holding on to our anger. This could lead to the sin of *hating your kinsfolk in your heart* instead of finding a way to say that I think you have gone astray. Our own failure to offer loving reproach can lead to holding a grudge and not being able to fulfill the central *mitzvah* of *Love your neighbor as yourself*.

Wandering Together

We need patience with ourselves and with one another to unlearn lifetimes of anti-fatness and to learn new ways of talking about bodies. It took forty years of roaming in the wilderness for the Children of Israel to make the transition from enslavement to homecoming. I would like to imagine, for those of us on a journey to embracing fatness, that—after all these years of twisted wandering—when we are ready to enter the promised land together, we may still have all kinds of mixed feelings about our own bodies, but we will have learned a new language, a truer vocabulary for bodies, for fatness, for love.

To my college boyfriend who broke up with me because I was fat and Jewish

I'm writing to express my gratitude to you. Truly, this is a love letter. Think of it as recompense for the fact that I only ever wrote searing breakup songs about you, which you would then have to listen to in public as I sang them from stage—in front of all of our friends—once we, once again, got back together.

What you said, that last time we broke up, was that we couldn't be together because there were differences between us. I was stubbornly mystified. Of course there were differences between us! Aren't there differences between any two people? So I asked you what differences you had in mind, and you said that you were neither fat nor Jewish.

Even at the time, you immediately tried to clarify that you meant that fat activism and Judaism were both really important to me and you could not fully participate in these parts of my life. But all I could hear was rejection and judgment. "And he's so stupid!" a mutual friend said, commiserating. "He's so stupid he thinks being fat and being Jewish have nothing to do with each other!" At the time, they connected for me only in that both my Jewishness and my fatness were seen as "too much." Both were out of the bounds of WASP acceptability.

But you are not stupid. Nor were you ending our relationship because you found my fatness or my Jewishness unattractive. A good fifteen years after we broke up, you called me out of the blue to make sure I knew that just because you were gay did not mean that what we had had was fake. You wanted especially to assure me that your physical attraction to me had been absolutely genuine. You made me stay on the phone with you until you were sure I believed you.

Looking back, since I started working on Fat Torah, I have been thinking of your words at our last breakup as prophetic. At a funeral, when I offer a *hesped*, I am trying to somehow express the Torah of the deceased. My eulogy seeks to evoke what this human being was born to say, to teach, to impress upon the world. What if you were seeing my big fat Torah years and years before I could see it myself?

One of the ways people in our circle of friends back then showed our love for each other was through mixtapes. Like other forms of sacred text, mixtapes are rich, but also richly obscure, giving the recipient endless opportunities for interpretation. It is said of Torah itself, "Turn it and turn it for everything is in it." That's what we did with those beloved cassettes, rewinding and replaying them again and again. Questions always outnumbered answers: Did you include this song just because you liked the sound of it, or were you trying to use it to say something that you could not say in your own words?

On one mixtape you made for me, you included the Waterboys' song "The Whole of the Moon." In my yearning to be loved and to be seen as special, I always imagined that you were casting yourself as the one who "saw the crescent" and me as the visionary who "saw the whole of the moon."

But what I want to offer here is the possibility that you were the one with the truer vision. You were like Bilaam, one of the Bible's non-Israelite prophets, who cannot know how he will prophesy until the words come out of his mouth. He's been paid to curse the

Children of Israel, but he is a true messenger of the Divine, and when he opens his mouth, the blessings flow.

At the time, I could only hear your words about my fatness and my Jewishness as curses. You were "outing" me as fat and Jewish; I was not ready. Not that these identities themselves were hidden, but I had not yet understood them as paramount to my life's work. It would take me decades to truly find joy in their confluence and to understand the fecundity in their interplay. So, in gratitude and beautiful hindsight, now I am the one singing the Waterboys' words about you:

I spoke about wings
You just flew
I wondered, I guessed and I tried
You just knew . . .
I saw the rain dirty valley
You saw Brigadoon
I saw the crescent
You saw the whole of the moon

Another central song for me in our college days was "Romeo and Juliet" by Dire Straits (because, of course, I insisted on preferring the original to the Indigo Girls' cover). "I dreamed your dream for you," sings Mark Knopfler, "and now your dream is real."

You dreamed my dream for me.

Now my dream is real.

Thank you.

6

Desiring Fat

Pudgy thighs, squishy belly, and cheeks! Oh, those cheeks. A bouncy chin or two or three. Countless inscrutable neck folds.

Anyone who has adored a fat baby's body knows the deep desire to tickle, nibble, and generally devour every delectable inch of them. My baby brother was born when I was three years and one month old, and I can still remember how very much I constantly wanted to bite him. Some of this was undoubtedly rivalrous aggression, but I am equally sure that some of it was just that he looked so irresistibly delish.

If you have ever found yourself having a hard time keeping your hands, or your mouth, off of such a baby—or for that matter a plump puppy or kitten—or even if you can merely sympathize with such an urge, then you know precisely how to love fat. You already know.

You know the silky velvet of it, like the loose fat skin just behind my Grandma Roz's elbows that she sometimes tolerated me playing with. You know the heft of fat and its warmth. You know its glorious undulation when it moves, and you know its solidity in stillness. You know its softness and its ready embrace.

So, please. Please go ahead and accuse me of "glorifying obesity" because—while that is not exactly how I would put it—I am here, guilty as charged, to glorify the sacred wondrousness of the fat body. I am here to let go of apology and explanation, to get free of comparison and justification, and to simply rejoice in adiposity, as we are born to do.

We fat people have been made to feel that we are both overly desirous—our hungers assumed to be out of control—and the embodiment of all that is undesirable. By tapping a deep—if too often hidden—well of fat love, we can dream together of a world where our true desires are honored, our hungers fulfilled, our bodies and souls well nourished, and our lovability a given.

I do not mean to imply that you are somehow required to love fat. Yes, I do believe we have an obligation to care for fat people—including our own fat selves, as best we can—just as we are called upon to care for all human beings. But you do not have to love being fat or being around fat people. Given the ocean of societal anti-fatness in which we all swim, I know how hard it is for many of us to love our own fat bodies and those of others, and this is no place for pretending otherwise. So, no, you do not *have to* love fat, but you are certainly, hereby, henceforth freely *allowed* to embrace both fat desiring and fat desirability. Because I also believe that at least some part of you already does.

Taste and Know

We can trust our own hungers—so much more than we are socialized to—to lead us to healing ourselves and this world. We are born knowing how to put things in our mouth and how to know whether they are what we want or not. As the psalmist urges, we can "Taste and know that YHVH is good" (Psalm 34:9). This is the Torah, the knowing, that is "not in the heavens . . . not beyond the sea . . . but very close, in your mouths and in your hearts" (Deuteronomy 30:12–14).

From the day we are born we have the power to take in or to spit out nipples, whether on a breast or a bottle. There are some babies and some caregivers who face genuinely difficult challenges with the technicalities of feeding. For many of them there is no small amount of heartbreak in this, and I do not want to minimize their pain. But most of us are born with a voracious "yes, please" and a vigorous "no, thank you." As we become older babies, we put all kinds of things in our mouths, often to the horror of our caregivers, tasting our way through the world and learning what we want more of and what we never want to put in our mouths again.

There are some things, certain medications come to mind, that taste awful but are actually what we need to ingest. And, of course, there are some things that taste good but are not right for us, either ever or simply inappropriate for the time or the place or our particular circumstances. Once I was drinking a beer and my nearly-two-year-old begged me to share it with her. I figured she would have one tiny sip and find out on her own that it was not for her. So, imagine my mortification when she tasted it, sagely nodded her curly little head, and soberly said, "More." There is, absolutely, a part of growing up that involves learning that what tastes good is not *always* good for us and that there are things that are good for us that do not taste or feel good.

We live, too, with a false dichotomy brought to us by anti-fat bias and diet culture that frames hunger as neatly divisible into "physical hunger" and "emotional hunger." When my first baby and I were learning to breastfeed, I once lamented to my husband that I could not tell when she wanted to nurse because she was physically hungry and when she wanted to nurse "just" for comfort. My husband quipped, "You can't tell for yourself; how are you supposed to tell for her?" Whacked out on postnatal hormones, I was deeply hurt at what I heard as an accusation that my own eating was at best unhealthy and at worst sinful. Relationship repair was achieved when he clarified that he meant that none of us can really tell the difference between eating for fuel and eating for comfort. I would add that none of us should expect ourselves to engage in this false binary as if our physical selves and our emotional selves could be peeled away from one another for examination on microscope slides. Both are legitimate reasons to eat. Desire is desire. It is not a formula for fueling some kind of machine. It is a wanting.

Fear of fatness is what makes eating for comfort problematic. Sure, having eating as your only form of comfort can be tricky, if you find yourself in a situation where you cannot reliably access the food you find comforting—for financial or logistical reasons or because there is something going on with you physically that keeps you from being able to eat it. It is also, theoretically, good to have a variety of ways to comfort ourselves. And anything we find soothing can sometimes be used in ways that keep us from making needed changes to our circumstances.

Thankfully, a growing number of clinicians—dietitians, therapists, and other medical professionals—understand how to help people heal from disordered eating without reinforcing anti-fatness. Sometimes we need the help of a trained professional to discern for ourselves the fine line between "soothing" and "numbing" or to sort out other especially difficult aspects of our relationship with food. But there is no more reason to restrict our eating for comfort than there is to restrict any other form of not immediately lethal self-soothing.

By and large we can, God willing, continue tasting our way through life, with our mouths but also with our other senses, with our inner knowing, with our hearts—trying out all kinds of different experiences and learning what we want more of and what we do not. And we can even learn that our tastes change and that we are well served by being able to sometimes taste again and know again, sometimes differently, what, and who, is good for us. We can, much more than we often allow ourselves to, follow our desire's lead.

When I was truly ready to leave a particular city I was living in but was tangled up in lists upon lists of intellectual pros and cons for staying or going, I found relief in birthing this song snippet:

It was my own heart I followed
into this heartbroke town
and I intend
to follow it out again

So far, my very best choices in life have been made by tasting and feeling my way forward, no matter how many lists and charts and spreadsheets I may have constructed in an attempt to make my decisions seem more rational.

Dieting and the Perversion of Desire

Somewhere around the age of five, I started learning that simply relying on my own desires was not allowed for me. I learned that my body was not the way it should be, that I could not trust the comfort of my small hands on my round belly, and instead had to believe those around me who made fun of the bigness of that belly or seemed worried at its roundness. And then I learned that everyone seemed to think that the way I was eating, tasting my way through the world, was also wrong. I learned that the things I loved to eat were not good for me or that the amount I wanted to eat was too much. That basic system of knowing when I was hungry and what I was hungry for was taken away from me, twisted in knots, and handed back to me distorted and unrecognizable.

My two grandmothers were easy to tell apart by the way they each made coleslaw. Grandma Roz, of the wondrous arm fat, made her coleslaw creamy and slick with mayonnaise. The shreds of cabbage were on the wide side, and the flavor was mild and soothing. Bubbe Ida's coleslaw featured thinner cabbage slices, no mayonnaise, fascinating caraway seeds, and a tart vinegar dressing—much more intellectually stimulating than it was emotionally comforting.

Once when I was maybe seven or eight years old, my Bubbe Ida put a plate of cookies down right in front of me at a meal with extended family and, in earshot of the whole gathering, fixed me with her birdlike gaze and said, "You don't want any of those, do you?" With over four decades of hindsight, I believe she thought she was making a devilishly smart joke. But small me did not get any such joke, and instead this scene is seared in my memory: the desired tasty thing put right in front of me, the knowing that she did not think I should have any, and then the barb that spoke to how contorted my own system of desire and satisfaction had already become. Did I want them? Who could even reliably sense such a desire when I already knew that I was not supposed to have them?

Here is how my whole framework of eating and hunger—and, indeed, desire more broadly—became profoundly disordered: the consistent resounding message that if you want it, it cannot possibly be good for you, and if someone tells you it's good for you, you have to accept it whether you like it or not. Your desire should become a signal of what you are *not* allowed to have. If you feel drawn to a particular food—or, for that matter, a particular person or a particular career choice—it is by definition not meant for you. Learn to suppress what you actually find tasty and try navigating the world instead by whatever will earn you the prize of being acceptable to others. To be wanted you must lose weight; to lose weight you must stop trusting your own wanting.

This warped architecture of desire has followed me for decades, well after I stopped actually dieting. While I feel I have a relatively healed relationship with food and with my body, I can still have moments when I feel stymied in trying to figure out what I actually want to eat. And beyond food and bodies, this twistedness continues to impact every aspect of life in which desire plays a role.

At one point in graduate school, I realized that part of my difficulty in making progress on my dissertation was stemming from the fact that writing a dissertation felt incredibly similar to dieting. Having rejected the latter as simply bad for me, I struggled with forcing myself through the former. So I took a two-page spread in my journal and labeled one column "dieting" and the other column "dissertating," in an attempt to come to terms with their similarities while praying that there was some difference between them that would make the degree doable.

Suppress your current desire in pursuit of a future goal. A checkmark in the dieting column and a checkmark under "dissertating."

Listen more to other people's ideas of what you should do and be than you listen to your own inner voice. Check. Check.

Focus on one goal to the exclusion of any others. Check. Check.

Restrict your socializing because it gets in the way of your goal. Check. Check.

Cut out more and more sources of actual pleasure in your life. Check. Check.

Let your own sense of what you actually want wither and die while you put all your energy into this commitment that promises a big payoff. Check. Check.

But then, the one tiny sliver of light shining from the far-off end of the dissertation tunnel, the saving distinction between dieting and dissertating scrawled in big letters at the bottom of the two-page spread: my sweet, sweet heart, I promise you, if you write this thing, if you can haul your ass up this mountain, YOU ONLY HAVE TO DO IT ONCE.

And somehow that promise was enough to pull myself through to the end of the PhD—that plus an incredibly supportive dissertation committee, a kick-ass therapist, friends who came through in the clutch, and parents who agreed to house me and do my laundry.

This became a mantra: *You only have to do it once.* I made a practice of standing on the shore of Lake Michigan, spreading my arms wide, imagining the dissertation already written, and belting out over and over again: "HalleluYah, the great storm is over. Lift up your wings and fly!"[1]

Dissertations can be finished or they can be quit. Dieting is almost never finished. Quitting is the only way out. For the vast majority of people who wish they were thinner, the great storm of trying to lose weight will never truly be over. Anyone who genuinely wants to live their whole life this way is, of course, welcome to. I am not here to dictate the free choices that anyone else makes in the hardly free context of intertwining webs of oppressive systems. But *HalleluYah*, what a blessing it is for me to never have to diet—or dissertate—again.

Yetzer Makes the World Go Round

It can be frightening to imagine letting our desires lead us. *Yetzer*, the desire drive in Jewish tradition, is often imagined in monstrous terms. While each of us is seen as having within us *yetzer hatov* (an inclination to do good) as well as *yetzer hara* (an inclination to evil), the term *yetzer* by itself is usually employed as shorthand for the latter: the desire to go astray. Our sacred texts and their interpreters offer countless examples of people struggling, or failing to struggle hard enough, with *yetzer*: having sex with inappropriate partners, breaking Shabbat, and yearning for pork. There is no question that desires that are unchecked by either morality or community can lead to great harm: physical, sexual, and emotional violence; abuses of power; bigotry and oppression. Yet, when properly channeled, seeking the satisfaction of our most basic desires—for food, for sex, for livelihood, for acceptance and recognition—is what makes life life.

The Talmud imagines *yetzer* as a fiery lion cub (BT Yoma 69b) that should be destroyed if it cannot be tamed. Once, while the Temple still stood in Jerusalem, the people wanted to eliminate *yetzer* entirely. After they fasted for three days and three nights, the lion cub emerged from the Temple's Holy of Holies. The people wanted to kill it right then and there, but the prophet Zechariah advised them instead to seal this *yetzer* cub in a container made of lead.

After three days of this confinement of desire, it was discovered that all the chickens in all the land had stopped laying eggs. Were it not for *yetzer*, we learn in another rabbinic text, no one would ever build a house, get married, have children, or even engage in commerce (Bereshit Rabbah 9:7). *Yetzer*, our basic desires, the wanting within each living thing, makes the world go round.

We are commanded (Deuteronomy 6:5) to love God with all our heart. The Hebrew form of "your heart" (*levav'cha*) in our verse has something curious in it. It is written with two of the same letter (the Hebrew letter *bet*) even though "your heart" could also be written with just one. Why this doubling of the letter *bet*? The Mishnah (Berakhot 9:5) offers that this doubling is there to teach us that we are commanded to love God with our *yetzer hara* as well as with our *yetzer hatov*. In other words, we are meant to love and to live with the wholeness of our desire.

Even now I feel hesitant writing about desire, worried that it is too much, that I am too much, still experiencing that nagging residual sense that if I *want* to write it this way, it must be wrong. Decades after giving up dieting, I remain afraid that my own desire—in this case, my desire to write about desire—might somehow be harmful. But desires themselves are never harmful. We should certainly consider the consequences of our actions in response to our desires, but the wanting, the hunger itself—feeling it, acknowledging it, owning it, even celebrating it—is always allowed.

Deprivation Is Not a Jewish Value

Judaism is not a tradition that values monasticism or asceticism; self-deprivation is approached with caution. Beyond the fixed fast days during the Hebrew calendar and a few other possibilities for fasting for special circumstances, depriving ourselves of food and drink is not traditionally smiled upon. Consider the case of the *nazir*, a person who takes a vow to refrain from drinking wine or grape juice, cutting their hair, or having contact with a dead body for a chosen period of time (Numbers 6:1–21). When the period of their Nazirite vow comes to an end, the *nazir* brings a sin offering.

The sacrificial rite had different offerings for different occasions or purposes. Why was the *nazir*, who presumably made their vow because they wanted to be especially holy, required to bring a sin offering and not just an offering of thanksgiving or some other kind of sacrifice? The rabbis of the Talmud (BT Nedarim 10a) have a rare moment of broad consensus when a number of them agree that a *nazir* is indeed a sinner because he caused himself suffering by refraining from drinking wine. The text goes on to expand this idea beyond the *nazir* and to declare that "anyone who fasts [unnecessarily] is called a sinner."

Though a person's body size is determined by a large number of factors, our culture's assumption is that fatness is a sure sign of "out of control" desire. Fat people are punished for our presumed desires regardless of what we actually want or don't want. I find it deeply healing and heartening to listen for the voices in Jewish tradition that have a much more straightforward, accepting approach to desire.

In addition to the rabbis' concerns about the *nazir* causing their own suffering, we learn in a different part of the Talmud (YT Kiddushin 4:12) that each of us will one day be held to account for everything that our "eye saw but [we] did not eat." *Halakhah* (Jewish law) certainly has a number of frameworks limiting what those of us obligated to *mitzvot* do with our bodies. Some of these have to do with morality or ethics, and others are nonrational (laws of *kashrut* being a prime example here). Again, the tradition is definitely concerned with the proper channeling of our desire into the world. Some of us find this approach restrictive in ways that are not healthy for us, and I am not offering a prescription here for what anyone else's relationship should be with this aspect of our tradition. What is clear to me, though, and clearly worth celebrating, is that we are meant to fully enjoy every permissible pleasure that this life has to offer us.

God Was Lacking Lack

Jewish mysticism imagines a time before the biblical creation story when only God existed in perfect infinity. God was only missing one thing: loving connection with another being. In this imagining, Divinity withdrew into itself the tiniest bit (*tzimtzum*) in order to make room for the rest of Creation: the human realm with its ongoing dance of hunger and satisfaction, wanting and finding, losing connection and seeking it once again.

In one variation of the blessing made after eating, we praise God as the one who creates "many souls and their lacks." Without our hungers, we could never experience the satisfaction of fullness. Without our wanting, how would we ever connect with ourselves, one another, and the Divine? From the moment we are born, hunger is the starting point for relationship: wanting, asking for what we want, giving to one another, enjoying our togetherness, love.

Eat and Be Satisfied

After I was done writing my dissertation, I went and stayed with friends in Berkeley, California, for several weeks. I bought a small bedazzled notebook and a tiny set of colored pencils. I would wander around the jasmine-scented streets, stopping occasionally to open my tiny notebook, pick a colored pencil, and write at the top of the page, "WHAT DO I WANT?" Then I would try to listen through the many layers of twisted-up expectations and prohibitions for one single true desire to bubble up.

And *HalleluYah*, sing praise to the Source of all life, desire did bubble up, the well was not dry. I wanted all kinds of things: to welcome music and songwriting back into my life, to go on dates, to eat yummy foods, to sleep as much as my body wanted to sleep. My desire was a blessed, unstoppable force, "my phoenix heart," as I would later describe it in song. Suppress it repeatedly and it gets harder and harder to sense or make sense of. Feed it well and soon it will rise again to lead me forward once more. "Many waters cannot quench love," sings the Song of Songs (8:7), "neither can the floods drown it."

To eat and feel satisfied, to desire and to have desire fulfilled, is a blessed situation. God is praised as the one who satisfies all creatures, implanting in us both desire and its fulfillment. Psalm 136, the Great Hallel, whose every verse ends with the refrain *ki l'olam ḥasdo* (for God's lovingkindness is endless), begins by praising God as the creator of all reality and then moves into a litany of praise for rescuing the Jewish people from slavery and from destruction. The psalm ends by praising God as the one who feeds every creature, "giving bread to all flesh." Nourishing ourselves—physically, emotionally, intellectually, spiritually—is a redemptive divine act. The sacred joy of Shabbat is marked by having an entire additional meal. When we feed ourselves, we imitate the God of whom our psalmist sings as "opening Your hand and sating to their pleasure all living things"[2] (Psalm 145:16).

The Calf and the Cow

Wanting and being wanted are symbiotic with one another, so intertwined as to be inseparable. We learn about this in Talmud (BT Pesaḥim 112a) when Rabbi Akiva is imprisoned by the Roman authorities for teaching Torah. His student Rabbi Shimon bar Yoḥai comes to visit him in prison and asks that he teach him Torah. Rabbi Akiva does not want to endanger bar Yoḥai further but understands his student's yearning for Torah from his teacher. He expresses this by saying, "More than the calf wants to suck, the cow wants to suckle." Any nursing parent, or any dairy farmer for that matter, can tell you that it is indeed incredibly painful to be ready to nurse and to not have any way to get the milk out. But more than this, Rabbi Akiva's yearning to teach speaks to the mutuality of hungering and satisfying hunger. Such a rebuttal to ableist and puritanical ideas of individualism and independence!

Wanting to be fed and being wanted go together. This goes for the desire for teaching and learning Torah as well as for any other kind of hunger. What if we imagined that our every desire was met in this universe by an equal and opposite yearning to fulfill our desire? What if our desire is an *indication* that somewhere, somehow, there is someone or something yearning to satisfy our hunger? Granted, this makes it understandable how painful it is when hunger goes unsatisfied. But it also allows us to imagine that our wantedness is contained in our wanting itself. I read "God is close to those who cry out" (Psalm 145:18) as closeness contained in the crying out for closeness. Wanting intimacy is an intimate thing.

Your Belly Is a Heap of Wheat

NAAFA was founded by thin, white heterosexual cisgender men who loved fat women and were appalled at the treatment their fat partners received at the hands of family members, employers, and doctors. When I joined NAAFA as a teenager, I was mortified by this history. My feminism and my fat liberation were completely intertwined, and it seemed wrong that the fat acceptance movement in its organized form was launched by men on women's behalf. I wanted to be desired, but I did not want to be objectified or seen as in need of saving. Recently I have been reexamining my cringing reaction to learning this history. In a world that sees fat people as simultaneously overly desirous and completely undesirable, fat attraction—a sexual preference for fat partners—is usually portrayed as a fetish, a matter of kink, or a joke; it is sent outside the camp of the "normal" range of acceptable desire.

Against this backdrop, and without letting go of the necessary critique of white male saviorism, there is still something beautiful to me about the fact that this particular body of fat acceptance is rooted in a love of fat people. This is no sterile or staid campaign for equal rights based on high principles so bland that we can all tepidly agree on them.

It is a messy, juicy, desirous embrace of fatness because we love fatness right down to a primal, eros-filled depth, at the core of our beings.

Desire for fatness sings out of the Song of Songs, which Rabbi Akiva describes as a textual "holy of holies," saying, "The whole world is not as worthy as the day on which the Song of Songs was given to Israel!" (Mishnah Yadayim 3:5). In this most beloved of biblical songs, filled with verses of two lovers celebrating each other's bodies and overflowing with yearning for one another, we hear this praise of the fat belly (Song of Songs 7:3):

Your navel is like a round goblet–
Let mixed wine not be lacking!
Your belly like a heap of wheat
Hedged about with lilies.

I hear in this ancient text an invitation to let our own creative juices flow in finding more and more words to describe the beloved fat body—our own and anyone else's.

Loving fat bodies can also call us to a more expansive love, a fattening of desire itself, rejoicing in the diversity of human form.

At a meditation retreat I attended some years ago, by the third or fourth day, being in silence with people I did not know was making me feel very exposed and vulnerable in my fatness. I could not rely, as I usually did, on the use of my voice to connect with people and to "prove" my worth. With words, I could make people laugh, impress them, or do whatever I needed to do to convince myself that they liked me. With only my silent body, I was frightened of their presumed rejection.

And then in one otherwise sleepy afternoon meditation session, in which dozens of us sat on our cushions trying to keep our eyes open despite having warm, full bellies after lunch, our meditation teacher suddenly looked up from her own cushion at the front of the room. Her words jolted us upright as she gazed out at us sitting in our many rows and said, "It's like I'm looking at a field of wildflowers." Tears streamed down my face as I returned my attention to my breath, sitting taller now that I had been reminded that I could be seen and appreciated in my uniqueness and that the wild variety of our bodies made us more and not less beautiful to behold.

Clinging to the Body

Our ultimate desire is the desire for life itself. We can learn what it means to love our bodies from traditions surrounding the reluctance of the soul to leave the body at the moment of death. Moses's soul was so resistant to the idea of leaving a body she had epically journeyed with for 120 years that she rebuffed the Angel of Death, who was sent to separate her from Moses's physical form. Finally, God Godself had to go and kiss Moses on the mouth so that his soul could go right from Moses back to God with no angelic intermediary (Devarim Rabbah 11:10).

The Zohar also describes how difficult it is for the soul to leave the body in death (Zohar 1:245a). Quoting a verse from the Song of Songs—"For love is fierce as death" (8:6)—this central text of Jewish mysticism imagines:

> For love is fierce as death—as fierce as separation of spirit from body. We have learned: When a human is about to depart from the world . . . the spirit moves through each member of the body . . . like a boatman without oars who is tossed up and down on the

sea and makes no progress. It then asks leave of each limb; and its separation is only effected with great violence.

I aspire to love my own fat body with just this fierceness, not because it is especially virtuous or is better or worse than any other body. I do not need to argue for or even prefer to have a fat body in order to desire to live as fully as I can in the only body that I have, the only life that I have. I offer this blessing: May I cling to this beloved body ferociously—letting its roaring desires continue to lead me—in honor of the journey we have already been on together and with the hope of many more roads to come.

Conclusion
Opening to the Beloved

"I was asleep," says the lover in the Song of Songs (5:2), "but my heart was awake. The voice of my beloved is knocking, saying, 'Open to me.'" In this holiest of holy texts, we catch a glimpse of the lover—long imagined as a stand-in for the Jewish people—snoozing away while the beloved (who is the Divine in this allegorical reading) is knocking at her door, pining to connect with her.

We have been, as individuals and as a society, largely asleep to the rupture, the deep wound that is anti-fatness. We have been willing to live in a world where people are judged, discriminated against, and laughed at for the size of their body. But I deeply believe that within each of us is a wakeful heart listening for the infinite possibility of another world knocking on the door.

In the text of the Song of Songs, the lover hesitates before opening the door to her beloved. In a tragicomic moment, she is concerned about whether she is dressed enough and whether she wants to get her washed feet dirty again. By the time she rises and reaches the door handle, her hands dripping with myrrh, her beloved is already gone. If you feel called to push out into a world that embraces all bodies, the time is now. For your own sweet self, for your fat friends and loved ones, for your sense of what is wrong with this world and what your part is in righting it, for the beloved within each of us and beyond us all, the time is now. If your wakened heart hears even a whisper of that divine knocking, the time is now.

The time is *now*. But how? Anti-fatness is woven so thickly throughout our lived realities that it is inescapable. It is within us, in our most casual and our most intimate interactions, in the media we are exposed to, and in our built environments.

There is, however, one good thing about the ubiquity of anti-fat bias: you can begin to unravel it by pulling—gently or urgently—on whichever strands are most easily within your reach. Or as my angry young self wrote in "The Bathing Suit Song":

You can have a little up-rising from wherever you're put down
So I start my revolution in my bathing suit
And I make my politics very, very personal.

Endless, if endlessly challenging, possibilities of how to answer this call await you and us all. It takes courage and smarts and humor. It takes whatever you've already got.

You may want to focus on healing your relationship with your own body. This work is quiet but holy. Finding the right therapist or other listening companion can certainly help and so can filling your social media feed with fat-positive words and images. You may find that working on "neutrality" toward your body is a better goal than expecting to go from self-hatred to immediately embracing everything about yourself. Maybe the best you can do in terms of your relationship with your own body right now is to just put the focus elsewhere, to concentrate on all the ways your life is more than your body. That's fine too.

Stubbornly difficult feelings about our own fatness need not, however, be obstacles to pushing back against anti-fatness in other ways. As I wrote in chapter 5, you can work on how you *speak* about your own body and other bodies regardless of your feelings. Fat-embracing words can bring healing to those around you even if you do not feel you have "perfected" your relationship with your own body. We do not have to finish the work of accepting ourselves to create a more caring world.

When you do speak, or post on social media, do so with the assumption that people who are fatter than you can hear you. When you use fatphobia to criticize public figures, even those who are in need of criticism, all the fat people can hear you. When you denigrate your own body, everyone with less thin privilege than you can hear you. If you find your own size unacceptable, what must you think of those of us who are larger than you?

You can work for a more fat-embracing world regardless of your own actual size. I have heard from a number of people wondering if they are "fat enough" to qualify for the work of fat liberation. Some have lost weight, intentionally or unintentionally, and wonder if there is still a place for them in fat activism. There most certainly is. It is important to try to center the voices of people on the larger end of the fat spectrum; all of us can practice allyship with people who are fatter than we are. But people of all sizes can call for an end to anti-fat bias. Indeed, in the category of "sad but true," you are more likely to be listened to if you are a thinner person advocating for the needs of fat people.

No matter our size, birthing a more fat-embracing world will require us to bring our whole selves—including a full awareness of our own particular combination of interwoven privileged and marginalized identities. Anti-fatness plays out differently in our lives depending on who else we are. Anti-fatness and anti-blackness have a particularly powerful and insidious interaction,[1] demanding that we aim for fat liberation that is also continually striving to be antiracist. We can also think about how fatness, and its stigma, interacts with gender, disability, sexuality, and neurodiversity.

In addition to trying to lift up the voices of those who come to the process of embracing fatness with bodies and perspectives that are different than our own, we also need to beware of falling into the trap of using our privilege in one area to try to combat our oppression in another. For example, as I mentioned in chapter 2, those of us with health measurements that allow us to "play the good fatty" run the risk of using ableism and healthism as a way to try to protect ourselves from anti-fatness. This is an understandable short-term survival tactic, but overall it can also contribute to strengthening oppressive forces in the world.

Moving from stuckness to freedom for every body really does mean all bodies, making sure that our fat activism is leading to liberation for all, not just getting our own sweet selves out of harm's way by pushing others aside and then locking the door behind us. Learning and teaching a Torah of fat liberation should ultimately mean learning and teaching a Torah that is itself fat: marbled throughout with the diverse experiences we each bring to it, audaciously abundant in perceptions and interpretations, bursting the bounds of what we previously understood.

One particularly powerful option for liberatory action is making amends to someone who has been harmed by your own anti-fat words or actions. Though it was nearly three decades ago, I will always be moved by the apology I received from a potential employer who passed me over for a job I really wanted because she felt a thinner candidate was better suited to the physical demands of the position; he turned out to be quite ill-suited. She told me how much she regretted her decision, and she was sorry for all the ways she had prejudged my abilities based on my size.

The words we choose not to speak can be equally as powerful as those we do. Maybe the best next step for you is to stop complimenting weight loss. Or you can try being mindful of how your putdowns of your own body sound to those of us in bodies larger than yours or to those of us with histories of disordered relationships with our bodies. Examine other ways that diet culture—with its incessant moralizing around food, bodies, and eating—is centered in your conversations and work toward decentering it.

Perhaps you are ready for a more concrete approach to pushing back against anti-fatness, like advocating for seating, clothing, and medical devices that work for people of all sizes—whether you yourself are fat enough to need access to them or not. You will almost certainly be received differently, and be taking significantly different risks, if you are advocating for your own fat self or if you are practicing allyship. In either case, it can be a very good idea to get support from a fat activist community if you plan on this kind of change making.

In fact, finding fat-embracing community can be an incredibly powerful and healing experience regardless of what fat activism you may be up for right now. You deserve to be with people—in real life or online—who accept you no matter your size, lift you up, share fat-friendly resources with you, and help you think through what you need to learn and unlearn in taking your next steps on this journey.

If you want to be active in the arena of law, you can check on how much, or how little, progress has been made where you live to make it illegal to discriminate against fat people. In the United States, as of this writing, NAAFA is hard at work to expand legal protections beyond the two states and eight cities that include body size or "personal appearance" in their anti-discrimination laws and codes. I hope the list will be much longer by the time these words reach you, but there is a good chance there will still be plenty of ways you can help in this area.

If you are a healthcare provider, you can stop using your patients' size as a stand-alone measure of how healthy they are, much less how worthy they are of your care and attention. If you are a clothing maker, you can start providing clothes in a wider range of sizes. If you work in a restaurant or a library or a school, you can look around your workplace to see how you might make fat people more physically welcome.

Maybe just reading this book has been the biggest challenge in embracing fatness that you are up for right now. Or maybe you are ready to challenge others to read it too—people in pain who need its soothing, people in power who need its call to make different choices, or people who just might be waiting for you to be the one to spark a conversation about anti-fat bias and how to confront it.

In short, there is no shortage of ways to practice healing the world's anti-fatness, within ourselves and beyond ourselves. The opportunities I have mentioned here are just a few examples. You know best what calls to you and what you are ready to put your energy into. You have the rest of your life to keep pulling apart the fabric of anti-fatness and reweaving a different world entirely.

• • •

When I was getting ready to release my second album, I wrote to Pete Seeger in the hope that he would agree to offer me a quote that I could include in my press kit—an actual physical folder of promotional materials to send out to folk festivals, radio stations, and other venues, back in the days when hard copies were seen as preferable to email attachments. I was pretty sure Pete would write back to me; luckily this was not a cold call. Pete knew of my existence from my years of working for Clearwater, the Hudson River environmental organization he had founded. Still, I knew him to be someone who did not dole out praise willy-nilly. I had no idea what he thought of my singing, and I was nervous, since he would definitely be honest about it.

After my weeks of waiting, his handwritten note arrived in the mail, his signature followed by its characteristic sketch of his banjo. His first sentence was reassuringly positive; he definitely said nice things about my singing. But the end of the quote caught me completely off guard. "Sing on, Minna," Pete had written, "bind this world together!"

I had been searching for a compliment, and what I got was a charge. Seeking his approval, I was given a mission, my Pete-decreed marching orders. Having a voice was all well and good, but only if I put it to the work of world healing. So, now I am passing this on to you:

You are beloved, exactly as you are.

Every body is.

Now get out there, however you can, and sing that to this waiting world.

Acknowledgments

Today I am dancing with gratitude.

My editor, Sandra Korn, asked me to write a different book than the one I had proposed to her, and I am so glad she did. She made both the process and the product of my writing more liberatory. This book has been through a number of iterations, and through them all, Dr. Rebecca Cory stood by the project, offering much-needed feedback and accountability. Thank you both for being this book's midwives.

Rebecca also convened a circle of first readers who read an early draft. Shoshanna Barnett, Rabbi Jay LeVine, and Rev. Tessie Mandeville: Your questions, insights, critiques, and cheerleading were invaluable to me.

The Fat Torah community has been a constant source of inspiration and support, reminding me of why this book needs to exist and championing it at every step of the way. In particular, I want to express how grateful I am to Emily Goodstein, Fat Torah's founding board chair, and Rachel Figurasmith, our current board chair and executive director. I feel so blessed to be in this work with you.

Thanks also to Fat Torah interns Emily Rogal and Elisheva Pripas, for your time and energy, for your leadership, and for your labor.

My *chevruta*, Rabbi Daniel Klein, gamely jumped into learning with me, helping me to develop a number of the themes in these chapters and to root them in our rich and beloved tradition of Jewish text. Rabbi Sharon Cohen Anisfeld's constant support of my evolving rabbinate has been a source of strength and creativity, freedom and growth.

Dr. Melila Hellner-Eshed let me sit at her feet as we edited the English translations of two of her books; my learning from her continues to be invaluable. Rabbi Ellen Lewis provided me with steady supervision, coaching me through writing blocks and encouraging me to bring more and more of myself to this work. Raizel Direnfeld-O'Brien, my kickboxing teacher, made space for me to truly embody the Torah that I am offering in this book, sometimes by punching things.

Speaking a truth that lots of people do not want to hear can be lonely work. I will always be grateful to the fat activists I have met along the way, from my earliest days as a NAAFA member to the folks who fill my social media feed today. Thank you for always letting me know that I am not alone.

My parents, Margaret and Mike Bromberg, and my mother-in-law, Diane Abrams, not only have been supportive of my work but have been a steadfast source of tangible help, especially in taking care of our children when "Imma has to teach" or when "Imma has another meeting."

Rabbi Alan Abrams, my beloved husband, has been my teacher and my partner in growing my understanding of the vital nexus of spiritual care and social justice. He sometimes bristles at being described as "resilient," but I have learned so much about resilience from him—as a writer, a rabbi, a parent, and a spouse.

Our sweet children have lived with the writing of this book for most of their lives. They have been my inspiration, my grounding, my loves.

I offer my deepest gratitude to the Beloved within each of us and beyond us all. May I awaken more and more to Your unending abundance.

Notes

Chapter 1

1. This was a direct (and brilliant) spoof of the "Lose weight now, ask me how" buttons worn by salespeople in the multilevel marketing diet scheme known as Herbalife.
2. Geneen Roth, *Feeding the Hungry Heart: The Experience of Compulsive Eating* (Bobbs-Merrill, 1982).
3. Geneen Roth, *Breaking Free from Compulsive Eating* (Bobbs-Merrill, 1984).
4. Jane R. Hirschmann and Carol H. Munter, *Overcoming Overeating* (Fawcett Crest, 1988).
5. Evelyn Tribole and Elyse Resch, *Intuitive Eating: A Recovery Book for the Chronic Dieter; Rediscover the Pleasures of Eating and Rebuild Your Body Image* (St. Martin's Press, 1996).
6. Jane R. Hirschmann and Carol H. Munter, *When Women Stop Hating Their Bodies: Freeing Yourself from Food and Weight Obsession* (Fawcett Columbine, 1995).

Chapter 2

1 I originally learned some of these framings of the meaning of *b'tzelem Elohim* at a rabbinic learning retreat with Rabbi Yitz Greenberg.
2 For more on pay disparities, see, for example, Aubrey Gordon, *What We Don't Talk About When We Talk About Fat* (Beacon Press, 2020).
3 K. E. Finn, C. M. Seymour, and A. E. Phillips, "Weight Bias and Grading Among Middle and High School Teachers," *British Journal of Educational Psychology* 90 (2020): 635–47, https://doi.org/10.1111/bjep.12322.
4 See chapter 3 for more on health and healthism.
5 This blog post on Cat's website is currently inaccessible due to her untimely death.

Chapter 3

1 Kathryn Post, "Fat Liberationists Celebrate Fat Bodies in Religious Community," *RNS*, December 6, 2021, https://religionnews.com/2021/12/06/fat-liberationists-celebrate-fat-bodies-in-religious-community/.
2 Robert Crawford, "Healthism and the Medicalization of Everyday Life," *International Journal of Health Services* 10, no. 3 (1980): 365–88.
3 See, for example, A. Stunkard and M. McLaren-Hume, "The Results of Treatment for Obesity: A Review of the Literature and Report of a Series," *AMA Archive of Internal Medicine* 103, no. 1 (1959): 79–85, https://doi.org/10.1001/archinte.1959.00270010085011. Ragen Chastain offers a timeline of studies confirming these results starting with Stunkard and McLaren-Hume's 1959 article (which itself reviews thirty years of prior research):

Ragen Chastain, "Who Says Dieting Fails Most of the Time?" *Weight and Healthcare Substack*, November 6, 2021, https://weightandhealthcare.substack.com/p/who-says-dieting-fails-the-majority.

4 Alison Fildes et al., "Probability of an Obese Person Attaining Normal Body Weight: Cohort Study Using Electronic Health Records," *American Journal of Public Health* 105, no. 9 (2015): e54–e59, https://doi.org/10.2105/AJPH.2015.302773.

5 Tracy L. Tylka et al., "The Weight-Inclusive Versus Weight-Normative Approach to Health: Evaluating the Evidence for Prioritizing Well-Being over Weight Loss," *Journal of Obesity* (2014), https://doi.org/10.1155/2014/983495.

6 Arthur Green, *Radical Judaism: Rethinking God and Tradition* (Yale University Press, 2010), 111.

Chapter 4

1 Emmanuel Levinas, *Totality and Infinity: An Essay on Exteriority*, trans. Alphonso Lingis (Kluwer Academic Publishers, 1961), 194.

Chapter 5

1 Minna Bromberg, "Your Belly Is a Heap of Wheat: A Torah of Fat Liberation," in *The Contemporary Reader of Gender and Fat Studies*, ed. Amy E. Farrell (Routledge, 2023), 325–36, https://doi.org/10.4324/9781003140665.

Chapter 6

1. From "The Great Storm Is Over" by Bob Franke.
2. This translation is from Robert Alter, *The Hebrew Bible* (W. W. Norton, 2018).

Conclusion

1. See Sabrina Strings, *Fearing the Black Body: The Racial Origins of Fatphobia* (NYU Press, 2019).

Works Cited

Alter, Robert. *The Hebrew Bible*. W. W. Norton, 2018.

Bromberg, Minna. "Your Belly Is a Heap of Wheat: A Torah of Fat Liberation." In *The Contemporary Reader of Gender and Fat Studies*, edited by Amy E. Farrell. Routledge, 2023.

Chastain, Ragen. "Who Says Dieting Fails Most of the Time?" *Weight and Healthcare Substack*, November 6, 2021. https://weightandhealthcare.substack.com/p/who-says-dieting-fails-the-majority.

Crawford, Robert. "Healthism and the Medicalization of Everyday Life." *International Journal of Health Services* 10, no. 3 (1980): 365–88.

Fildes, Alison, Judith Charlton, Caroline Rudisill, et al. "Probability of an Obese Person Attaining Normal Body Weight: Cohort Study Using Electronic Health Records." *American Journal of Public Health* 105, no. 9 (2015): e54–e59. https://doi.org/10.2105/AJPH.2015.302773.

Finn, K. E., C. M. Seymour, and A. E. Phillips. "Weight Bias and Grading Among Middle and High School Teachers." *British Journal of*

Educational Psychology 90 (2020): 635–47. https://doi.org/10.1111/bjep.12322.

Gordon, Aubrey. *What We Don't Talk About When We Talk About Fat*. Beacon Press, 2020.

Green, Arthur. *Radical Judaism: Rethinking God and Tradition*. Yale University Press, 2010.

Hirschmann, Jane R., and Carol H. Munter. *Overcoming Overeating*. Fawcett Crest, 1988.

Hirschmann, Jane R., and Carol H. Munter. *When Women Stop Hating Their Bodies: Freeing Yourself from Food and Weight Obsession*. Fawcett Columbine, 1995.

Levinas, Emmanuel. *Totality and Infinity: An Essay on Exteriority*. Translated by Alphonso Lingis. Kluwer Academic Publishers, 1961.

Post, Kathryn. "Fat Liberationists Celebrate Fat Bodies in Religious Community." *RNS*, December 6, 2021. https://religionnews.com/2021/12/06/fat-liberationists-celebrate-fat-bodies-in-religious-community/.

Roth, Geneen. *Breaking Free from Compulsive Eating*. Bobbs-Merrill, 1984.

Roth, Geneen. *Feeding the Hungry Heart: The Experience of Compulsive Eating*. Bobbs-Merrill, 1982.

Strings, Sabrina. *Fearing the Black Body: The Racial Origins of Fatphobia*. NYU Press, 2019.

Stunkard, A., and M. McLaren-Hume. "The Results of Treatment for Obesity: A Review of the Literature and Report of a Series." *AMA Archive of Internal Medicine* 103, no. 1 (1959): 79–85. https://doi.org/10.1001/archinte.1959.00270010085011.

Tribole, Evelyn, and Elyse Resch. *Intuitive Eating: A Recovery Book for the Chronic Dieter; Rediscover the Pleasures of Eating and Rebuild Your Body Image*. St. Martin's Press, 1996.

Tylka, Tracy L., Rachel A. Annunziato, Deb Burgard, et al. "The Weight-Inclusive Versus Weight-Normative Approach to Health: Evaluating the Evidence for Prioritizing Well-Being over Weight Loss." *Journal of Obesity* (2014). https://doi.org/10.1155/2014/983495.

About the Author

Rabbi Dr. Minna Bromberg is passionate about bringing her three decades of experience in fat activism to writing, teaching, and change-making at the nexus of Judaism and body liberation. She founded the organization Fat Torah in 2020 with the aim of smashing the idolatry of weight stigma and deploying Jewish tradition to build a world that embraces all bodies. Rabbi Bromberg received her doctorate in sociology from Northwestern University in 2005 and was ordained at Hebrew College in 2010.